Praise

in earth as it is in heaven

Praise and Worship
in earth as it is in heaven

ANNE MURCHISON

WORD BOOKS
PUBLISHER
WACO, TEXAS

All Scripture quotations, unless otherwise noted, are from the King James or Authorized Version of the Bible. Quotations marked RSV are from the Revised Standard Version of the Bible, copyright 1946, 1952, © 1971, 1973 by the Division of Christian Education of the National Council of the Churches of Christ in the USA. Quotations marked NASB are from the New American Standard Bible, copyright © 1960, 1962, 1963, 1968, 1971 by The Lockman Foundation.

Quotations taken from *The Pursuit of God* by A.W. Tozer and *Worship —The Missing Jewel of the Evangelical Church* by A.W. Tozer are used by permission of Christian Publications, Inc., Harrisburg, PA 17105. All rights reserved.
Quotations taken from *God's Best Secrets* by Andrew Murray are used by permission of Zondervan Publishing Company, Grand Rapids, MI 49506. All rights reserved.

ISBN 0–8499–2938–5
Library of Congress catalog number: 81–51008
Printed in the United States of America

89801239 FG 9876543

This book is dedicated to

THE LORD GOD ALMIGHTY

to

Ann Rosenberg
Olen Griffing
Shady Grove Church
Clint

to

all of those who have beating within them
the heart of David . . . a heart after God

Contents

Foreword

God has placed the subject of praise and worship, which this book covers so eloquently, as a top priority in my life. For several years I have felt that the **church** was to receive this message, and I am so thankful that He has chosen His vessel, Anne Murchison, to share that message with His people.

Her first book *Milk for Babes*, is the best I have ever read for learning about the person, Jesus, and answering those questions which so many new believers encounter. Now, *Praise and Worship . . . In Earth As It Is in Heaven* takes us on into new dimensions and communication with Him.

Anne is not writing from head knowledge, she is writing from experiences in worship. I have watched her grow into a beautiful flow of Davidic praise and worship and I know that she loves Jesus, she loves you, and the desire of her heart is that you, as a believer in Him, come to experience this same worship and praise.

David was a man after God's own heart. May God grant this same heart to us.

Olen Griffing, Pastor
Shady Grove Church
Grand Prairie, Texas

Preface

I enjoy praising the Lord for many reasons, one of which is that I am being obedient to His Word, and in obedience I am fulfilled. In this book, Anne has set forth many of the principles of praise and the scriptural reasons for praise being both obedient and fulfilling.

Be fulfilled. Praise the Lord.

Clint Murchison, Jr.

Acknowledgments

In gratitude . . .

First to the Lord of Glory, the King of Kings, the Mighty One of Israel, who created the heavens and the earth, who created all things for His pleasure, and whose pleasure is knowing and being known by us and communing with us through His Word, prayer, praise and worship. He is truth. He is the author of truth and particularly the truth contained in these pages and also the faith of the heart out of which all of this has flowed. To Him be the glory!

To the Body of Christ, a wonderful thing when it functions as it was created to do and be. The term Body of Christ is one that gets tossed around so loosely at times that we have lost the impact of what it really is—the living, breathing, visible expression of the invisible Lord. To those members of Christ's body who have ministered to me on the truths of God contained in this book, either personally or through their books, my warmest and deepest thanks, especially . . .

My beloved pastor, Olen Griffing, whose greatest desire is to see God's children solidly established in *all* truth and worshiping the Lord with all our hearts, minds, souls and strengths, in spirit and in truth. Much of what is in this book was learned in spirit and in truth through this dear brother.

My precious servant and dear friend, sister in Christ and

prayer partner, Ann Rosenberg, whose praise and worship life sparked me to jealousy and a deeper pursuit of God. Much of the truths in this book were taught to me by her as the Lord revealed them to her.

My church, Shady Grove, in Grand Prairie, Texas, for it is there that I learned how to enter into corporate worship and about the power that is manifested in its midst.

A. W. Tozer, Andrew Murray, Graham Truscott, and the host of other members of the Body of Christ who have ministered to me on the importance of praise and worship to the believer and to God.

Pat Wienandt, my editor and good friend, and Floyd Thatcher, Vice President and Editorial Director of Word, Inc., also my good friend, for their loving response to me and to this book and for their wisdom and understanding in the writing and rewriting of it.

And always the fruit of my labors are shared by Clint, my beloved husband and prayer partner, who is one flesh and one spirit with me, who encourages me in all I do for the Lord, especially through his prayers in my behalf, whose gentleness and tenderness and trust give me a great sense of freedom and peace and security, and who graciously shares me and my time for the sake of the Kingdom of God.

Personal from Me to You

This book in no way has been written as an indictment against anyone who does not agree with its content. It is rather a matter which flows forth from my heart and has brought a new and greater dimension to my relationship with my Heavenly Father and a deeper reverence for the Lord God Almighty, the Creator of the universe. The subject of this book, praise and worship, as I believe you will discover, has its very roots in God Himself.

However, one evening as I was sharing this very precious subject with friends who have not participated in praise and worship as outlined in this book, the question arose, "Does God love us commensurate with our obedience and good works?" Specifically, with reference to the spiritual principles of praise and worship, the focus of this book, does the Lord love those who are obedient to these truths more than those who see no need for them in their lives? The answer is **absolutely not!** But the more we walk in obedience to **all** truth, the more the reality of God's love will break through and permeate our lives and hearts, and the greater our capacity to perceive and receive His love will be. The Bible clearly reveals that praise and worship are the primary vehicles for entering into communion with God and the revelation of His glory. If you study this book with an open heart, I believe God will confirm this to you, just as He has to me.

It is in the fertile soil of a tender, abiding heart of integrity toward God, a heart that **desires** to walk as much as one is able, in total surrender **daily**, where the fruit of the Holy Spirit, the very character and personality of God, begin to come forth in abundance in our lives (John 15:4, 8). Therefore, let us press on to learn the importance of entering into His gates with thanksgiving and into His courts with praise each day of our lives.

This is an exciting subject and one that has been hidden away for many years. I believe you will be surprised and delighted! If as you read, God touches your heart with the truth of His Word, stop to respond to Him. Take time to thank Him and praise Him and worship Him. Let this book begin to minister to you and give birth to praise and worship toward God.

Introduction

LUKE 10:38–42: "Now it came to pass, as they went, that he entered into a certain village: and a certain woman named Martha received him into her house. And she had a sister called Mary, which also **sat at Jesus' feet, and heard his word.** But Martha was **cumbered about much serving,** and came to him, and said, Lord, dost thou not care that my sister hath left me to serve alone? bid her therefore that she help me. **And Jesus answered** and said unto her, Martha, Martha, **thou art careful and troubled about** *many things:* **but one thing is needful: and** *Mary hath chosen that good part,* which shall not be taken away from her."*

February 12, 1976, I began the most exciting adventure a human being can ever know, but on that day I had no perception of what was happening in my life. On that day, I surrendered my life and will to the Lord Jesus Christ, not knowing or understanding what that meant, but coming to Him broken, hopeless and wanting to die. I had run out of clever ideas. I had realized the fulfillment of all my hopes, goals and dreams and that had not brought me the elusive happiness I had pursued all of my life. Why *not* try Jesus?

I don't want to presume that you know my testimony, nor do I want to tell it in this book for it has been told in my first book,

---

*Throughout this book, all emphasis and all parenthetical comments within Scripture passages are the author's, unless otherwise noted.

Milk for Babes; but briefly, Jesus took a life that was bruised and battered, meaningless, hopeless and "plum" run out of ideas about where to turn next, and gave it purpose, meaning, hope, enthusiasm, and direction. In short, because of Jesus, quite some time ago I surpassed all of my hopes and dreams for the potential of my life and am now far beyond what I ever hoped to be. So much for my expectations, huh? Having been created in the image of God, we have *no* idea what the enormous potential of our lives is.

The revealed truth of God's Word has given me answers for my life, and the results of those answers have overflowed to touch the lives of many people, who I am sure have also touched the lives of many people to give purpose and meaning and fulfillment to others.

And that is the exciting adventure I mentioned at the beginning. Jesus makes a difference that lasts . . . forever. And He never ceases to make a difference if we are open to letting Him make that difference.

I was and am always seeking and asking God to change me, to sift the undesirable, lumpy parts of me out of the way, to strengthen my weaknesses in the fiery furnace, and I've discovered that God loves to respond to prayers of this nature. For these are prayers of longing and yearning to be like Jesus.

In the summer of 1979, I began to realize that my prayer life was not all that it should be. For three and a half years I had gotten by on a hit-and-miss basis with prayer and personal Bible study, and the Lord began to work in my heart to convict me of this sin. Though I had participated in three Bible studies a week and prayed in all of them, though I prayed frequently with personal friends almost daily over the telephone or in person, I had no "alone" time for the most important person in my life on a daily basis, and my growth, though steady, was not satisfactory.

It was at that time that several books that had been sitting on my shelves quite some time began to tickle my curiosity and interest. They were books on prayer, *The Ministry of Intercession* by Andrew Murray, *Rees Howells, Intercessor* by Norman Grubb, and two books by S. D. Gordon, *Quiet Talks on Prayer* and *Quiet Talks on Power*. But behind the interest and curiosity was a book

I had read by Paul Billheimer, *Destined for the Throne*, who had quoted the Gordon books considerably. Did these books ever make me thirsty to enter into the service of prayer! Little did I know at the time that God was using this desire for service to draw me into a deep, abiding, intimate relationship with Him that grows and changes with every day.

And so the great adventure took on a new dimension as I began to set my alarm clock to get up at 6:00 A.M. to pray. At the same time, my prayer partner, Ann Rosenberg, was telling me of her own quiet times that certainly added fuel to the fire of desire burning within me. She was spending great quantities of time with the Lord each morning in praise, worship and prayer, and God was responding to her ministry to Him.

Little did I ever realize when I began to take this step of obedience to God that He would respond to me, even me, in such a magnanimous way. In fact, He is so longing for each one of us to seek Him, to seek to know Him with all of our hearts.

It wasn't easy. My mind drifted a lot, I grew restless and fidgety, but I persevered. Applying a principle Andrew Murray mentioned in his book, I called out to God to anoint my prayer times. I asked Jesus, the great Intercessor, and His Holy Spirit to help me through the difficult times, and the faithfulness of God was mighty. And I still apply this principle as I come before the throne of God each day. I recognize my own frailties and inability to pray as I should. I proclaim my total dependence upon Him Who created me and Who ordained praise, worship and prayer. And I begin.

And God has honored my efforts. He has seen my heart and known my longings to know Him, the One Who has made such a difference in my life. I discovered that I could have continued in my Christian walk just as I was—saved, walking in the Spirit, knowing many blessings and being a blessing to many because of Him—and never have really known **Him**. It is in the knowing of Him that I found the true abundant life. I could have continued to know **about** Him, thinking I knew Him, and never have known Him. And yet my heart knew something was missing, and God responded to my hungry heart. He can be counted on to reveal not only the need in a hungry heart but the way to fill the need.

This book is a result of those humble beginnings and it is submitted to you, my reader and friend, in humility. It is the overflow of a heart too full to contain all that the Lord has revealed and continues to reveal to me about Himself. Much of what I have learned is inexpressible, as it is about anyone with whom you have an intimate relationship. But this is not just someone! This is God! And my finite mind cannot in any way express what He has revealed to me about Himself. You will have to venture on into knowing Him for yourself if you have not already begun. If you have not begun, I hope God has already used these few paragraphs to make you thirsty, just as He used the writings of Paul Billheimer to make me thirsty in the summer of 1979.

Even perfect knowledge of Hebrew and Greek and study of the perfect written Word of God will not supplant knowing the True and Living God intimately. Knowing anyone takes quality time alone with that person, sharing oneself and listening as the other shares. It is the same with God.

This book explores two of the essential components of that alone time with God, and though knowing God is an enormously profound and vast subject and there are many components in the progressive process of knowing Him, the Bible devotes the majority of its wisdom to this subject—praise and worship.

In spite of this fact, most of us have somehow missed out of the truth of praise and worship. A. W. Tozer has written a pamphlet, "Worship—The Missing Jewel of the Evangelical Church," which in essence says that all of creation is fulfilling its purpose except for man, **who was created for worship.** I will be quoting from this pamphlet, but I highly recommend that you read it for yourself in its entirety.

If you are hungry and thirsty for God, press on, my friend.

ISAIAH 5:13: "Therefore my people are gone into captivity, because they have no knowledge: and their honourable men are famished, and their multitude dried up with thirst."

I am prayerful that this book will help you find some answers.

Laying a Foundation

Before we get to the heart of this book, I feel very strongly that it is essential to lay a foundation. I have learned that, since spiritual growth is endless, we often must grow out of or beyond what we have learned at our mother's knee. We must also often grow beyond our pastor, minister or priest and beyond our church doctrines, for God is limitless. My own role models are three spiritual giants, Joy Dawson, A. W. Tozer and Andrew Murray, and yet I hope that I have not limited God to the dimensions of their faith, great as it is or was. I say this in all humility, because, if I ponder the reality of growing beyond these people of great faith with eyes of sight, it seems impossible. It is only when I meditate upon God and His infinite, eternal, awesome, mighty goodness and greatness in the fear of Him and with eyes of faith that I feel comfortable with believing Him for it. "All things are possible with God." I say these things, of course, to those who are eager, as I am, to grow into all God has for them, to those who have a heart like David—a heart after God.

Before I could grow beyond the limits of my pet doctrines and traditions, I learned that several things had to happen in my life. I believe these things may help you too and provide important groundwork for discovering the many exciting truths of praise and worship. These things will be found under the next three chapter headings: Choose Life! (p. 20); Where Am I? Where Do I Want to Be? (p. 28); and Who, Not How! (p. 47).

19

Choose Life!

1 CORINTHIANS 8:1: ". . . Knowledge puffeth up . . ."
DEUTERONOMY 30:20: ". . . HE is thy life. . . ."

The battle between man and God has been raging since Eve decided that the tree of knowledge of good and evil would make her "like God" (Gen. 3:5, RSV), that it was "good for food, and that it was pleasant to the eyes, and a tree to be desired to make one wise . . ." (Gen. 3:6).

It was God Himself who gave us the choice—to obey or not to obey, for one. Or from another vantage point, to choose His way (the tree of life) or our way (the tree of knowledge of good and evil). Or, another way of saying it would be He gave us the choice of Him or "self."

GENESIS 2:9, 16–17: "And out of the ground made the Lord God to grow every tree that is pleasant to the sight, and good for food; the tree of life also in the midst of the garden, and the tree of knowledge of good and evil. . . . And the Lord God commanded the man, saying, Of every tree of the garden thou mayest freely eat: But of the tree of the knowledge of good and evil, thou shalt not eat of it. . . ."

God's heart's desire is that we choose Him. He is life! Had not God given us that choice, our love toward him would have been merely perfunctory and would not have been of real meaning to Him. He longs for passionate lovers of Himself, not robots! Just like you and just like me. Hence the two trees represent those choices. If we choose the tree of life, we choose Him, which is life. If we choose to disobey God's command and partake of the tree of knowledge of good and evil, we choose death.

The lost of the world have, knowingly or unknowingly, consciously or unconsciously, chosen the tree of knowledge and consequently have chosen death. But many Christians **also** choose the tree of knowledge, and in a spiritual sense they are choosing death.

Now don't get me wrong. I am not saying that Christians lose their salvation for choosing the tree of knowledge, but what I am saying is that knowledge for the sake of knowledge, even Bible knowledge, which is knowledge of good, is not where life is. It is only the knowledge of God Himself that can give "life" to knowledge He is the source of all knowledge. But all too many of us are, it seems to me, on "head trips," and this does not bring life spiritually. Our minds can be changed without our hearts being changed.

I have found in my personal pilgrimage that Christianity involves more than a changed mind. It is a changed heart—a circumcised heart—and only God Himself can do that.

EZEKIEL 36:26: "A new heart also will I give you, and a new spirit will I put within you: and I will take away the stony heart out of your flesh, and I will give you an heart of flesh."

DEUTERONOMY 30:6: "And the **Lord thy God** will circumcise thine heart, and the heart of thy seed, to love the Lord thy God with all thine heart, and with all thy soul, that thou mayest **live.**"

Paul addressed himself to this subject of head knowledge versus heart knowledge.

1 CORINTHIANS 2:1–5, 9–12: "And I, brethren, when I came to you, came not with excellency of speech or of wisdom, declaring unto you the testimony of God. For I determined not

to know any thing among you, save Jesus Christ, and him crucified. And I was with you in weakness, and in fear, and in much trembling. And my speech and my preaching was not with enticing words of man's wisdom, but in demonstration of the Spirit and of power: **that your faith should not stand in the wisdom of men, but in the power of God.** . . . As it is written, Eye hath not seen, nor ear heard, neither have entered into the heart of man, the things which God hath prepared for them that love him. But God hath revealed them unto us **by his Spirit:** for the Spirit searcheth all things, yea, the deep things of God. For what man knoweth the things of a man, save the spirit of the man which is in him? even so the things of God knoweth no man, but the Spirit of God. Now we have received, not the spirit of the world, but the spirit which is of God; that we might know the things that are freely given to us of God."

A. W. Tozer expresses the same concern in his book, *The Pursuit of God.* "There is today no lack of Bible teachers to set forth correctly the principles of the doctrines of Christ, but too many of these seem satisfied to teach the fundamentals of the faith year after year, strangely unaware that there is in their ministry no manifest Presence, nor anything unusual in their personal lives. They minister constantly to believers who feel within their breasts a longing which their teaching simply does not satisfy. . . . The truth of Wesley's words is established before our eyes: 'Orthodoxy, or right opinion, is, at best, a very slender part of religion. Though right tempers cannot subsist without right opinions, yet right opinions may subsist without right tempers. There may be a right opinion of God without either love or one right temper toward Him. Satan is a proof of this.'

"Thanks to our splendid Bible societies and to other effective agencies for the dissemination of the Word, there are today many millions of people who hold 'right opinions' probably more than ever before in the history of the Church. Yet I wonder if there was ever a time when true spiritual worship was at a lower ebb. To great sections of the Church the art of worship has been lost entirely, and in its place has come that strange and foreign thing called the 'program.' This word has been borrowed from the state and applied with sad wisdom to the type of public service which now passes for worship among us.

"Sound Bible exposition is an imperative must in the Church of the Living God. Without it no church can be a New Testament church in any strict meaning of that term. But exposition may be carried on in such way as to leave the hearers devoid of any true spiritual nourishment whatever. For it is not mere words that nourish the soul, but God Himself, and unless and until the hearers find God in personal experience they are not the better for having heard the truth. The Bible is not an end in itself, but a means to bring men to an intimate and satisfying knowledge of God, that they may enter into **Him**, that they may delight in **His** presence, may taste and know the inner sweetness of the very **God Himself** in the core and center of their hearts.

"The whole transaction of religious conversion has been made mechanical and spiritless. Faith may now be exercised without a jar to the moral life and without embarrassment to the Adamic ego. Christ may be 'received' without creating any special love for **Him** in the soul of the receiver. The man is 'saved,' but he is not hungry nor thirsty after God. In fact he is specifically taught to be satisfied and encouraged to be content with little.

"The modern scientist has lost God amid the wonders of His world; we Christians are in real danger of losing God amid the wonders of His Word. We have almost forgotten that God is a Person and, as such, can be cultivated as any person can. It is inherent in personality to be able to know other personalities, but full knowledge of one personality by another cannot be achieved in one encounter. It is only after long and loving mental intercourse that the full possibilities of both can be explored.

"In the living breathing cosmos there is a mysterious Something, too wonderful, too awful for any mind to understand. The believing man does not claim to understand. He falls to his knees and whispers, 'God.' The man of earth kneels also, but not to worship. He kneels to examine, to search, to find the cause and the how of things. Just now we happen to be living in a secular age. Our thought habits are those of the scientist, not those of the worshipper. We are more likely to explain than to adore."

I hope you will forgive the above long quote and the one that follows. A. W. Tozer and Andrew Murray are not only men whom I greatly respect and admire and who are examples to me of the kind of Christian life I long for and pray for, but they are also men deeply respected by most of the Christian community and these quotes support strongly what I am saying regarding the tree of life and the tree of the knowledge of good and of evil. A point as important and complex as this one must make an impact on our lives, and it always helps to hear it from several points of view.

Quoting from *God's Best Secrets* by Andrew Murray: ". . . in the Church of Christ the gifts of human learning and wisdom speedily asserted themselves, instead of that entire dependence upon the Holy Spirit, of which Christ had spoken. And with that learning came, as a natural consequence, the exaltation of self, and the whole difference became the question between Pride, in the power of human learning and wisdom, and Humility, in the absolute dependence on the teaching of the Holy Spirit.

"Much of our religion is ineffectual, because people accept the truths of God's Word with the intellect, and strive to put them into practice in their own strength, but it is only the Holy Spirit that can really reveal divine truth to us. A young student in a theological seminary may accept the truths of God's Word as head knowledge, while the Word has little power in his heart to lead to a life of joy and peace in the Lord Jesus. Paul teaches us that when we read God's Word, or meditate on it, we should pray: 'Father, grant me the spirit of wisdom and revelation.' As we do this each day we shall find that God's Word is living and powerful, and will work experience in our hearts: God's commands will be changed into promises. His commands are not grievous, and the Holy Spirit will teach us to do lovingly and joyfully all that He has commanded."

Knowledge for the sake of knowledge, even Biblical knowledge, brings pride and arrogance and a barren spiritual life. The tree of life brings deep communion with God, life, and humility, for no man can be in the presence of God and feel proud and arrogant.

David understood this as well as any man of God in the Bible. He certainly expressed it more. He loved the Word of God passionately and wrote about it as a lover writes home to mom and dad about the girl of his dreams and theirs: "The law of the Lord is perfect, **converting the soul:** the testimony of the Lord is sure, **making wise the simple.** The statutes of the Lord are right, **rejoicing the heart:** the commandment of the Lord is pure, **enlightening the eyes.** The fear of the Lord is clean, **enduring forever:** the judgments of the Lord are true and righteous altogether. **More to be desired are they than gold, yea, than much fine gold: sweeter also than honey and the honeycomb"** (Ps. 19:7–10).

Those are not words spoken from the intellect. No. Those are words spoken directly from the heart of a man deeply in love with the Lord, whom he clearly knows and understands very well.

The law David loved is spiritual (Rom. 7:14) and is spiritually discerned (1 Cor. 2:14) . . .

ISAIAH 11:2: "And the **spirit of the Lord** shall rest upon him, the spirit of **wisdom** and **understanding,** the spirit of **counsel** and **might,** the spirit of **knowledge** and of **the fear of the Lord."**

. . . and though the above verse pertains specifically to the Messiah within the context that it is written, it pertains to every believer in Jesus Christ, because we have been given that same Holy Spirit within us. . . .

ROMANS 8:11: "But if the Spirit of him that raised up Jesus from the dead dwell in you, he that raised up Christ from the dead shall also quicken your mortal bodies by his Spirit that dwelleth in you."

. . . and we are heirs of God and joint heirs with Christ (Rom. 8:15–17) in all things (Heb. 1:2) through the same Holy Spirit.

It is only when we come to the Lord with broken, contrite hearts, when we come to Him at an end of ourselves and our own understanding (or the understanding of others that has been imparted to us) and begin to desire to be taught truth by the Lord, that the spirit of God can begin the deep work within us of Isaiah 11:2—to give us the heart of David reflected in Psalm 19:7–10. Scripture reveals that this really all begins with the fear of the Lord, which is to hate evil (disobedience in anything).

PROVERBS 8:13: **"The fear of the Lord** is to hate evil: pride, and arrogancy, and the evil way, and the froward mouth, do I hate."
PROVERBS 1:7: **"The fear of the Lord** is the beginning of knowledge. . . ."
PROVERBS 9:10: **"The fear of the Lord** is the beginning of wisdom: and **the knowledge of the holy** is understanding."

Therefore, let us pray for the fear of the Lord. Let us seek together God's wisdom and understanding, and I am certain that what God has promised, He is also able to perform (Rom. 4:21).

DANIEL 10:21: "But I will shew thee that which is noted in the scripture of truth. . . ."
JEREMIAH 33:3: "Call unto me, and I will answer thee, and shew thee great and mighty things, which thou knowest not."
JOHN 6:63: "It is the spirit that quickeneth; the flesh profiteth nothing: the words that I speak unto you, they are spirit, and they are **life."**
There are two reasons I have devoted so much space, effort and thought to this chapter. First, I believe it is only when truth is imparted to us by the Spirit of God that it becomes light and life, and second, it is only when truth is taught to us by the Holy Spirit that there can be a breakthrough in our personal doctrines and traditions. The spiritual truths of praise and worship were certainly something I had not heard before and they were counter to some of what I had been taught, or at least counter to my ingrained, cultural heritage and traditional understanding of Christianity. Therefore, it was something I

overlooked when I came to study the Bible. It's easy to skip over even an important truth.

Human beings are funny. We don't like change, even when it is for the better, and we will resist it with all that is within us. It is the nature of the Adamic ego to do so. Yet God understands our struggles and His Holy Spirit is our Helper, our Enabler. Even so, God will not violate our will. He tenderly works in our lives until we are willing to change, though some of us are simply never willing.

Shall we press on together in this great adventure of knowing and growing in the Lord?

DEUTERONOMY 30:19–20: "I call heaven and earth to witness against you this day, that I have set before you life and death, blessing and curse; therefore **choose life,** that you and your descendants may live, loving the Lord your God, obeying his voice, and cleaving to him; for that means **life** to you (Moses is speaking to Old Testament **believers)** and length of days . . ." (RSV).

There is blessing in obedience . . . and life.

O Lord, how we long to grow in your truth. We long for you to give us new hearts . . . hearts after you. We pray for the spirit of wisdom and revelation in knowledge of you, dear Lord. We pray that you would reveal the riches of the glory of your inheritance in us and the surpassing greatness of your power to us. Give us wisdom, understanding, counsel, might, knowledge and the fear of the Lord. We praise and magnify your wonderful name and give thanks to you for your precious grace. It is in the wonderful name of Jesus that we pray. Amen.

Where Am I?
Where Do I Want to Be?

PSALM 101:6: "My eyes shall be upon the faithful of the land, that they may dwell with me; He who walks in a blameless way (of integrity) is the one who will minister to me" (NASB).

As I was writing the previous chapter on heart knowledge versus head knowledge, it became so clear in my spirit that we must definitely be taught by the Holy Spirit, we must have changed hearts, even more than changed minds, and yet that is not the ultimate destiny in our spiritual lives. Rather the changed heart is the vehicle to growth that leads us into the blameless way of integrity and into worship of the Lord.

The Bible not only reveals where we belong. It also reveals a pattern for walking with integrity of heart and attaining and maintaining our place there. Our ultimate destiny is to commune with God before His throne (Exod. 25:22, Heb. 4:16) and our pattern for reaching and staying in communion with Him there is found in the priestly walk through the tabernacle of Moses.

This fellowship and communion and the blessings and anointings that flow forth in us as a result thereof (which we will study in greater detail in a later chapter when we study the river in Ezekiel 47), are our full inheritance as believers in Jesus Christ. Yet, as I wrote earlier, many of us fail to claim it. It's a bit like inheriting a trillion dollars and never taking possession of it. If we live in poverty but have a trillion dollars in the bank, we definitely have not claimed our full inheritance. I had no awareness of my full Christian inheritance until recently. Even now I am only beginning to learn about it and claim it. Indeed, levels and degrees of understanding and revelation can be discerned every step of "the way" of integrity, and on every plateau of maturity.

A few years ago I received a set of tapes by Derek Prince entitled "The Way Into The Holiest." I learned from those tapes that God has given us a pattern for our Christian walk, and since discovering it has been so beneficial to me, I thought it would be helpful to share my understanding of it here in a very simplified way.

For any reading this book who might not know, the tabernacle of Moses was the literal dwelling place of God and the place of ministry and worship for the Israelites as they traveled through the wilderness into the promised land. The pattern for its construction was given by God to Moses on Mount Sinai down to the most minute detail (Exod. 26–27). A very deep and wonderful study can be made of these instructions, but for the purposes of this book we will touch on only a few aspects. Through them I have gained a much greater understanding of God, His Word, and my relationship with Him. I pray they will do the same for you.

In the diagram shown on page 31, I have drawn the three areas of the tabernacle and labeled them **A, B,** and **C.** The pieces of furniture are numbered from one to seven, and the entrances are marked **i, ii,** and **iii.** (These areas, entrances and articles of furniture represent many things, many more than I will enumerate here.) In the study of the three areas and their entrances we learn of the progressive understanding of the Word of God and our relationship with Him, and with the study of the furnishings we learn of the progressive **process** of growth in that relationship.

Notice that we begin from the part of the tabernacle **(A)** opposite that from which God does. We come in the only way we can and move into the Holy of Holies **(C).** God's priorities are revealed in the giving of the pattern for the tabernacle, for He begins with instructions for the Holy of Holies and works from there **out.** Our highest priority and greatest desire should be the same as God's.

The tabernacle's triune structure (Outer Court, Holy Place and Holy of Holies) corresponds to the triune nature of God (Father, Son and Holy Spirit) and the triune nature of man (body, soul and spirit). The three entrances correspond to the three aspects of John 14:6, i, Jesus the Way; ii, Jesus the Truth, and iii, Jesus the Life. As we enter "The Way," the only entrance into the tabernacle (no one comes to the Father [C] but by Jesus, The Way [i]), please make a mental note of our ultimate destination, which is area C, the area of the Father and the place where the Presence (Glory) of God dwells. Even though we may never have had a full understanding of this, God is always working to woo and draw us there, and this is why the changed heart is so essential. We cannot get there with a changed mind alone, for the flesh is weak. A changed mind may **know** it needs to grow, it may **know** it is doing wrong, but it is only as we enter into the Holy Place **(B)** and our wills are there submitted to the control of the Holy Spirit, that our heart is changed.

But let's now enter The Way. As we come in, we are face to face with the brazen altar **(1)**, or altar of burnt offerings, which typifies (represents or symbolizes) the cross upon which Jesus died. This is where the animal sacrifices were offered up for the sins of the Old Testament believer once a year. After the believer laid his hands upon the head of the animal and repented and confessed his sins, the animal was slain, its blood was sprinkled upon the altar, it was washed with water and offered up upon the fires of the altar, all in the manner prescribed by God. These sacrifices are Old Testament types of the substitutionary death of Jesus for our sins, and the brazen altar is an Old Testament type of the cross. It is important to mention that the blood was also sprinkled upon the altar of incense **(5)** in the Holy Place **(B)** and the mercy seat **(7)** in the Holy of Holies **(C;** see Heb. 9:11–14 and 10:19). It is important because it is the blood of Jesus that gives Christians access and let us never forget it! Without the sacrifice of Jesus, no amount of effort could get us to our ultimate destination **(C)**.

As the priest leaves the brazen altar, he goes to the laver bowl **(2)** and washes himself. The laver bowl typifies several things. It typifies water baptism. It also typifies the holy

WHERE AM I?
WHERE DO I WANT TO BE?

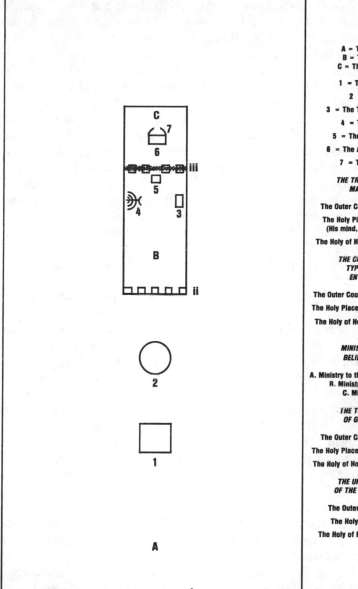

A = The Outer Court
B = The Holy Place
C = The Holy of Holies

1 = The Brazen Altar
2 = The Laver
3 = The Table of Shewbread
4 = The Lampstand
5 = The Altar of Incense
6 = The Ark of the Covenant
7 = The Mercy Seat

*THE TRIUNE NATURE OF
MAN TYPIFIED:*

The Outer Court = Body (of man)
The Holy Place = Soul (of man)
(His mind, will and emotions)
The Holy of Holies = Spirit (of man)

*THE CHRISTIAN WALK
TYPIFIED BY THE
ENTRANCE TO:*

The Outer Court = Jesus, the Way (I)
The Holy Place = Jesus, the Truth (II)
The Holy of Holies = Jesus, the Life
(III)

*MINISTRIES OF THE
BELIEVER/PRIEST:*

A. Ministry to the lost and newly saved
B. Ministry to the brethren
C. Ministry to God

*THE TRIUNE NATURE
OF GOD TYPIFIED:*

The Outer Court = God, the Son
The Holy Place = God, the Holy Spirit
The Holy of Holies = God, the Father

*THE UNDERSTANDING
OF THE WORD TYPIFIED*

The Outer Court =   Logos
The Holy Place = Rhema
The Holy of Holies = Communion

Scriptures. Ephesians 5:26 states that we are "washed of water by the word," meaning that the reading of The Word literally washes us and changes our minds. The laver bowl was made of the mirrors of brass of the women of the Israelites' camp. In the Bible, brass always symbolizes judgment. Therefore, we can see that in our washing by the water of the word not only are we judged but we are given a standard for judging our own behavior, though our understanding of the word at the laver bowl is mostly historical, intellectual, and ethical in scope.

The Outer Court's lack of covering and its openness to the natural light of the sun, moon and stars typifies our reading and understanding of the Word of God through our natural senses, without the wisdom, enlightenment and revelation of the Holy Spirit. This understanding of the Word is called Logos. It relates to those things perceived by our senses, and therefore to the body of triune man, and not to his soul and spirit. This is a "faith knowledge," as opposed to "revelation knowledge." The Outer Court also correlates to the ministry of Jesus, the Son of the triune God, in the life of the believer.

A Christian who has come only as far as the brazen altar or the laver bowl is a carnal (unregenerate) Christian who knows Jesus as Savior but not as Lord. Drawing an analogy with our worldly friendships gives us a clearer perspective. Such friendships usually exist on one of three levels. There are acquaintances, close friends, and intimate relationships. For the Christian who is still in the Outer Court, Jesus is a mere acquaintance. He is **The Way** to salvation.

Next the priest enters into the Holy Place **(B)** of the tabernacle through the entrance which represents Jesus the Truth **(ii)**. The Holy Place corresponds to the ministry of the Holy Spirit of the triune God in the life of the believer, for even though as believers we receive the Holy Spirit at the altar of sacrifice **(1)**, it is in the Holy Place that we begin to manifest the Spirit-filled life, coming under the Lordship of Jesus Christ. The believer who appropriates the spiritual truths in the Holy Place comes to know Jesus—in terms of worldly relationships—as a close, personal friend. He is **The Truth** of salvation.

The Holy Place also corresponds to and deals with the soul of triune man, which is also triune in its makeup, consisting of will, intellect and emotion. The three articles of furniture in the Holy Place very beautifully correspond to those three areas of man's soul.

The first article of furniture at which the priest stops is the table of shewbread **(3)**, which typifies the Lord's supper—communion with God and brethren. On the table of shewbread are twelve loaves of bread. The bread has to do with the will of the believer, for just as the bread is prepared, so must the will of man be prepared. The wheat must first be ground into flour and then it must be sifted to remove all "lumpy," undesirable parts. It must be stirred, kneaded and pounded and then molded into shape and baked in a hot oven. Man's will must be submitted to the same spiritual process. It must be crushed, ground up, sifted as fine flour, beaten, molded and baked in the fires of purification. It must relinquish all of its carnal desires and all rights and be submitted to the will of God. I am not saying here that the will must be annihilated, for then you would have asceticism. What I **am** saying is that the will must cease functioning independently, allowing the soul to become a vessel for the spirit. It is the **independent action** of the will that must be destroyed, not the will itself. This is where we learn to say, "Yes, Lord," "Whatever **you** want, Lord." Until this occurs in the life of a believer, he cannot go on with God. He cannot receive true wisdom and revelation in the knowledge of God (Eph. 1:17) at the lampstand **(4)**, and he cannot be a worshiper in spirit and in truth (John 4:23) at the altar of incense **(5)**. This process is called "dying to self" or to "flesh."

From the table of shewbread we move to the lampstand **(4)**, which has to do with the intellect of the believer, for this is where the believer moves from head knowledge to heart knowledge, to wisdom and revelation in the knowledge of God mentioned in Ephesians 1:17. The Holy Place and the Holy of Holies are contained in the tabernacle, a covered building in the back half of the Outer Court, and the lampstand is the only source of light in the Holy Place. The oil in the lampstand is symbolic of the Holy Spirit, and the light produced here is obviously symbolic of the supernatural enlightenment of the eyes of the mind by the Holy Spirit. This is called Rhema, or revelation knowledge. Rhema is received through the quickened word of God, through a still small voice within us, through dreams and visions, through circumstances and through ministering angels. It is only as our will is surrendered to God that we can have discernment and wisdom to know which voices, visions, and dreams are of God, and which are not.

The next item of furniture is the altar of incense (5), which has to do with the emotions of the believer. This is where the priest offers up to God the sweet incense burned in fire to the Lord. The fire on this altar typifies intensity, purity and passion of the soul. The incense speaks of devotion, made fragrant by the test of fire. The smoke arising from this fire typifies the adoration expressed in praise and worship. These elements, intensity, purity, passion, devotion and adoration are all necessary to our emotions for spiritual praise, worship, and prayer. If man's will is not submitted unto God, the praise and worship of the believer offered here at the altar will be fleshly in nature as opposed to spiritual.

The altar of incense is the place of transition into the Holy of Holies, for it is in the release of prayer, praise and worship that we are then free to enter into the dwelling place of God. Without it (and the blood), there is no access to His Glory. And that is the subject of this book—scriptural praise and worship in spirit and in truth. This is something there is almost no teaching on in the whole Body of Christ, though it is taught in some churches. Yet it is essential to communion with God.

As we enter into the Holy of Holies (C), we carry with us the sweet, smoking incense of praise and worship before the mercy seat (7). There is absolutely no light there in the Holy of Holies except the radiating Glory of God. There are two pieces of furniture which look like only one, because one rests upon the other. The mercy seat (7) rests upon the Ark of the Covenant (6). There are two arks mentioned in the Bible and both of them are types of Christ. Noah's ark is symbolic of the *believer in Christ* (protected from the wrath and judgment of God, which is death, and identified with His death in the waters of baptism, among other things). The Ark of the Covenant symbolizes *Christ in the believer*. Let's see why.

Inside the Ark there are three items: the golden pot of

manna, Aaron's rod that budded, and the tables of the covenant (Heb. 9:4). The golden pot typifies the divinity of Christ and the manna typifies Jesus as the bread of life, and through this bread we have union and communion with the Father. For Jesus said, "I have life by union with the Father. He who believes in me will have life by union with me as I have union with the Father, and by that union with me, he will feed upon me. I will be the hidden manna of your heart, and on that manna you will feed day-by-day" (see John 6:48–51, 57).

The tablets of stone contained in the Ark typify the law of God hidden in the heart of Christ. We can plainly see that it is not we who keep the law, but Christ **in us** keeping the law (Ps. 40:7–8 and Gal. 2:16).

Aaron's rod that budded typifies authority, which comes through testimony and revelation. Jesus said, ". . . All power is given unto me in heaven and in earth" (Matt. 28:18). He also gave that authority to believers. "Behold, I give unto you power to tread on serpents and scorpions, and over all the power of the enemy: and nothing shall by any means hurt you" (Luke 10:19). It is only Christ **in us** that gives us this authority. It is nothing of ourselves. Let's review it. Christ **in us** means (1) union with the Father (the golden pot with manna), (2) authority and revelation (Aaron's rod that budded) and (3) Christ in us keeping the law (the tablets of stone).

Further, the tablets also typify the unchangeable, eternal law of God, specifically worship, because we are now in His Presence. The manna typifies fellowship and communion with God. Aaron's rod that budded typifies the revelation of God's character and personality. These three important necessities to the life of the believer can only be manifested in the Holy of Holies.

We will see these same three types also revealed in the mercy seat (7), which typifies the atonement of Christ. "Being justified freely by his grace through the redemption that is in Christ Jesus: Whom God hath set forth to be a propitiation through faith in his blood, to declare his righteousness for the remission of sins that are past, through the forbearance of God" (Rom. 3:24–25). "Propitiation" literally translates from the Greek as "mercy seat." The mercy seat symbolizes the mercy of God.

Apart from the shed blood of Jesus Christ, there is no eternal mercy.

On each side of the mercy seat there is a cherub. They are symbolic of the same worship, fellowship and communion with God, and revelation of God's character and personality as the golden pot of manna, the tablets and Aaron's rod which are found inside the Ark in the Holy of Holies. The attitude of the bodies of the cherubim are attitudes of worship (their wings are bowed). Their faces are toward one another, which symbolizes fellowship. Hebrews 9:5 says they are the cherubim of glory shadowing (covering) the mercy seat. The Greek word for "glory" is *dŏxa* and it translates "dignity, glory (glorious), honor, praise, worship." These cherubim cover the mercy seat with praise and worship and glory and honor. And this is where God said He would meet with you and with me. "Where the wings meet and the faces meet, there will I reveal my Glory to you" (see Exod. 25:20–22). There He will manifest His presence. That is revelation!

So we have these three important necessities in the life of the believer—(1) worship, (2) fellowship and communion with God, and (3) revelation of God—presented twice, once in the Ark of the Covenant and once in the mercy seat. The double emphasis stresses God's desires and priorities for us.

And here we also have the ultimate corollary lessons . . . in the Holy of Holies. In terms of worldly friendships, we enter and begin to grow in a deep, personal, union and intimate relationship and communion with the Heavenly Father of the triune God. Here the spirit of triune man enters and begins to grow in "The Life." Here we find profound rest and communion with God.

The veil, the entrance into the Holy of Holies and "The Life," iii, separated the Holy Place from the Holy of Holies. Only the High Priest entered through this veil into the Holy of Holies, and then only once a year on the Day of Atonement.

This veil, according to information available to us from the Talmud, was woven approximately four inches thick. It was very heavy. But at the moment of Jesus' mortal death, a truly supernatural act of God caused it to be torn in two (see Matt. 27:51–52). And it was the death of Jesus and this rending of the veil that gives us as believers access to the throne of God and "The Life" (Heb. 4:16, 10:19–20). What depth of understanding this adds to those words spoken by Jesus, "I am come that they might have life, and that they might have it more abundantly" (John 10:10). This rending of the veil by the death of Jesus gives every believer access to "The Abundant Life."

The rent veil not only typifies or represents the death of the mortal body of Jesus, but it also typifies the death to sin of the believer in Christ (Gal. 2:20). But as noted earlier, though every believer now has access to the throne of God, few of us come. Many of us are content simply to be "saved." We never move beyond the cross of Jesus (which is the brazen altar). Some of us are content with the Logos only, the history, the faith knowledge, the "thou shalts" and the "thou shalt nots." Many are content to remain carnal, doing their own thing. (And there is little recognizable difference between a carnal Christian and a nonbeliever.)

It is my understanding that to come under the full Lordship of Jesus, to know Him as more than the "man who got us into Heaven," it is important that we appropriate the spiritual truths of each piece of furniture in the Holy Place. We are to submit our will to Him, participate in the Lord's Supper, and come to the Holy Spirit of God at the lampstand for enlightenment, truth, and guidance and then faithfully walk in obedience to the wisdom we receive there. We then come to the altar of incense and enter into the ministry of praise and worship of God, and supplication, prayer and intercession for all saints. It is at this place of transition that we move into the Holy of Holies and come before His throne. We can omit any part of the spiritual process, but if we do, we cannot come into the Glory of His Presence, for the application of every truth contained in each of the seven pieces of furniture is essential to the obedience of God. And we need continual, daily application and appropriation of these truths in our lives in order to **maintain** our place in His presence. We may be able to fool people, and many of us do quite successfully, but we can never fool God, and the depth of our relationship with Him is directly reflected in our desire and willingness to obey His leading and apply these truths in our personal lives.

It is important here to say that there are many truths I have not mentioned regarding the Holy Place **(B)**. But I am confident that as you walk with a tender heart of faith, open to the Lord, you have in this book the essential truths for Him to lead and teach you the others. It is also quite important to emphasize again and to caution that we are still and always talking about levels of understanding and degrees of maturity throughout our spiritual lives regarding **all** spiritual truths. Proverbs 4:18 says, "... the path of the just is as the shining light, that shineth more and more unto the perfect day." It is an ongoing process for the diligent seeker. In the Bible I see one verse that clearly delineates the levels of spiritual understanding: 1 Corinthians 2:9 says, "... Eye hath not seen, nor ear heard [the outer Court **(A)**; the body (or senses of man); Logos, Jesus The Way], neither have entered into the heart of man [the Holy Place **(B)**; soul (of man); Rhema, Jesus The Truth], the things which God hath prepared for them that love him [the Holy of Holies **(C)**; spirit (of man); communion, Jesus The Life]."

For instance, I have come to a much deeper revelation of Christ's death on the cross. The agony of Gethsemane has pierced my heart deeply. My awareness of what He suffered when He took upon Himself the wrath of God for the sins of the entire world has grown and is more of a reality to me. For as I have grown in grace and understanding, He has revealed in a small way what He suffered, and He has called me to take the wrath of the sin of another person against me upon myself, even when I have not sinned. Especially when I am innocent of any wrongdoing. The sting of another's sin against me is particularly severe then. To take that wrath upon myself, to forgive, to love, to bless, to pray for one who has wronged me deeply—to do so without retribution, without self-pity ... to turn the other cheek ... to say as Jesus said, "Father, forgive them, for they know not what they do" ... **that** is a tiny bit of what Jesus suffered. And to experience the grace of God in the midst of this suffering! That is a deeper revelation of the death and resurrection of Jesus.

Another example of levels and degrees of understanding and revelation is my first book, *Milk for Babes*. As I contemplate the truths of God revealed to me in that book, I find myself wishing

I could write it all over again, because of the deeper levels of understanding of those truths within me. But, of course, then the Lord reminds me that that was a book written for babes by a babe. As my husband commented in the foreword to that book, most Christian books are too complicated for babes. So I thank the Lord for His great blessing and wisdom, and I "press on, forgetting those things which are behind (past accomplishments) and reaching forth unto things before me."

An interesting thing happens in studying the tabernacle of Moses: it opens up the Bible in a miraculous way to new levels of understanding and discovery. It was, I believe, eternally intended by God to do so, and I feel sure that a Christian cannot understand the Bible in all its depth and beauty without a basic understanding of the tabernacle of Moses. Fifty chapters of the Bible are dedicated to it—thirteen chapters of Exodus, eighteen chapters of Leviticus, thirteen chapters of Numbers, two chapters of Deuteronomy and four chapters of Hebrews. This does not include numerous references scattered throughout the Bible. Much of what is written in the Bible is crystallized and clarified with an understanding of the tabernacle, and that, I'm convinced, is God's divine intention and design.

Moses' tabernacle is a pattern of the heavenly tabernacle (see Heb. 8:1–5; 9:11, 24). The Book of Revelation gives a complete picture of the tabernacle in heaven where God dwells eternally. So it is quite natural for Jesus in particular, and the Bible in general to relate and equate spiritual principles to it. It certainly confirms divine inspiration of the Scriptures to see this continuity throughout a book that was "penned" by at least 40 authors over a period of approximately 1600 years.

Another example, and a good one, of a deeper revelation of the Scriptures through the tabernacle is that famous conversation that Jesus had with Nicodemus. That is where Jesus coined the spiritual phrase, "born again." Early in my Christian life, I came to understand that phrase to mean that we must each individually be born "from above" by the power of the Holy Spirit into God's family, just as we each were individually born "of the flesh" into our earthly families. Just as Jesus was conceived within the womb of Mary by the power of the Holy

Spirit, He must be conceived within us by that same Holy Spirit. But I believe that the Lord has further opened up to me those references in John 3 through a deeper understanding of the tabernacle.

If the Christian who enters into the Holy of Holies (C) enters into worship, fellowship and communion with God, and into revelation of His character and personality, I believe he or she has entered into the spiritual kingdom of God (also called the kingdom of heaven) right here on earth in a very real way. For by examining the scriptures in Revelation (which we will do in the next chapter) where we are given glimpses of heavenly activity, we discover that that is exactly what the hosts of heaven are involved in: worship, fellowship and communion with God, and the revelation of His character and personality. So for just a moment, look at this with me. It is wonderful! Jesus said that we must be born again to **see** the kingdom of God (John 3:3). If we enter into the outer court through The Way (i) and come to the brazen altar (1) and accept Jesus as our Savior, we are born again . . . we are born from above by the Holy Spirit of God. We can **see** the tabernacle which contains the Holy of Holies some 75 feet away as we enter The Way (i), but we have not yet **entered** into the Holy of Holies and the kingdom of God.

Let's look further. Jesus did not stop there. In John 3:5 He said, ". . . Except a man be born of water and of the Spirit, he cannot **enter** into the kingdom of God." Continuing with the tabernacle as our frame of reference, I believe we can see a great mystery unfold. Except a man be born of water (at the laver bowl [2]) and of the Spirit (the complete ministry of the Holy Spirit provided in the spiritual truths of the Holy Place [B]), he cannot, according to Jesus' words, **enter** into the kingdom of God (in the Holy of Holies [C]).

We **can** individually, spiritually enter the kingdom of God here on earth. This is God's number one priority for His children. This is not only revealed in the dual emphasis of worship, fellowship and communion with God, and revelation of God in the Ark of the Covenant and in the mercy seat. It is also revealed in the order given in the pattern for construction of the tabernacle. The Ark and the mercy seat are the first things mentioned in the pattern. "And there I will meet with thee, and I will commune with thee from above the mercy seat, from between the two cherubim which are upon the ark of the testimony (covenant), of all things which I will give thee in commandment unto the children of Israel" (Exod. 25:22).

We do **not** have to wait until we die and go to heaven to enter into the kingdom life. As we enter into praise and worship (at the altar of incense), we can then enter into the Holy of Holies and come into the presence of God and His kingdom, in earth as it is in heaven. Jesus said, ". . . The kingdom of God is within you" (Luke 17:21).

Certainly I am not saying that every reference to the kingdom of God and heaven can be appropriated today, for I believe many do pertain to the millennial kingdom that is to come when Jesus returns. However, Jesus said His kingdom was not of this world (John 18:36) and that we, His disciples, are not of this world either (John 17:16, 20). Therefore, I do earnestly believe many truths of the kingdom are for today, even though many of us have never understood this. And one of the ways the Lord will open these truths up to us is through praise and worship.

We cannot remain babes in Christ and be partakers of the divine nature. We cannot remain babes and enter into the spiritual kingdom of God here on earth. It is important to let Jesus grow up within us so that we may grow up in Jesus. We must go on to maturity! As we walk the blameless way of integrity, we can be sure we will enter into the kingdom of God to minister unto Him (Ps. 101:6).

This new understanding of the Holy of Holies in the tabernacle relating and equating it spiritually to the kingdom of God, makes the following verses ever so delicious.

LUKE 17:21: "The kingdom of God is within you."

MATTHEW 6:33: ". . . seek ye first the kingdom of God, and his righteousness; and all these things shall be added unto you."

LUKE 11:2: ". . . Thy kingdom come. Thy will be done, as in heaven, **so in earth**" (see also 1 Cor. 4:20; Rom. 15:17; and Col. 1:13).

So you see? There are continual shifts and changes in the levels and degrees of our spiritual understanding if we are pressing on with the Lord. There are also, often, shifts in our doctrinal and theological beliefs because of this. That is where I believe most denominational and nondenominational doctrines fall short. They are systems created by man and therefore limited in scope. God is limitless and we must keep on growing. That does not mean we are always to give up on our denomination or "non" denomination. (Indeed, the Word of God clearly indicates we are to have a commitment to a local church.) It simply means we must recognize it for what it is and not be limited by it. There is no such thing as "arriving," for we all "come short of the Glory of God" (in the Holy of Holies, Rom. 3:23), and we are all involved in the process of learning and growing.

We must repent, confess our sins and take up our crosses . . . daily. We must be cleansed and renewed by the washing of the water of the word . . . daily. We must surrender our wills to God, be desirous of and open to the teaching and leading of the Holy Spirit, especially when it contradicts what we have previously been taught or what we believe is truth but is error, and we must enter into the ministry of praise, worship and prayer . . . daily. There is no such thing as resting on our laurels.

An important thing I must share with you is that I don't always reach the Holy of Holies. I don't believe any of us can achieve that ideal. Sometimes I stay in the outer court. Sometimes I just never quite get around to the altar of incense. It is so important to remember that "there is no condemnation for those in Christ Jesus." I am not always going to do everything I should. I am not always going to be in perfect harmony with the Lord, because I still dwell within an earthen vessel that is subject to slips and falls. What is important to remember is that God loves me just the same. I am free in Christ to fail, and sometimes I think that is as important to know as it is to know that God desires our obedience. Otherwise we do slip into the sins of legalism (the letter of the law), judgment and condemnation, and self-righteousness. However, I don't want to be misunderstood on this point either. Let me state emphatically that I am not saying we can sin habitually and grow. We cannot! And that is the difference in a heart of integrity—a heart that wants to obey and regrets deeply any disobedience.

God has given us a pattern, and it is up to God to grow us up. It is not a theological system. He doesn't want us to make a denomination out of it. It is His pattern for the way for the seeking heart to enter into deep communion and fellowship with Him. I reiterate that all He desires of us is a willing heart, not a "perfect" heart. For instance, before I ever heard Derek Prince's tapes on the Tabernacle of Moses and saw the spiritual truth of it unveiled in such a beautiful way, God had already imparted most of those truths to me. What this teaching did was to confirm work the Lord had previously done in my life and the direction in which I was currently being led. And what is so marvelous to me about the Word of God is that all those wonderful truths are hidden there in the Tabernacle of Moses. God is so consistent. So you can relax. Let go and God will do it. He will lead you. He will enable and empower you. He will bring you into the Holy of Holies if you so desire and are willing to press on.

It is worth it, my friend. It is worth it! This is where intimacy with the Lord begins, much as two lovers, whispering sweet somethings to one another, sharing lots of wonderful things you can never know apart from the Holy of Holies. This is where the deep, intimate, love relationship develops. The relationship for which we all truly yearn. This is where our spirits begin to come fully alive in Christ. And the purpose of this book is to open up the reality and the avenues of this for all of us. Truly, I am learning even as I have written this book, much as I did with *Milk for Babes*.

I feel certain that book must have been written under an anointing of the Holy Spirit of God. I, of myself, surely was not capable, as a two-year-old Christian, of writing it. I had come as far as the lampstand in the Holy Place. In my personal evaluation from the tabernacle study, I knew Jesus as The Truth, but I had not approached the Altar of Incense. I was experiencing the reality of wisdom and revelation in the knowledge of Him at a certain depth. But in the summer of 1979, I knew I had to press on and I began to set aside time on a daily basis for communion with God, adding to my spiritual walk a private, special time for Him which consisted of praise, worship and prayer. It was through this obedience and release of praise and worship that I entered into the Holy of Holies to worship at His throne.

I began to attend Shady Grove, where I learned to participate in corporate praise and worship in a way I had never known before, and the fruit of these new ingredients in my spiritual life began to be manifested. New things began to happen in my life. Many of them are unspeakable. There are not words to express them. But some of them are very tangible.

In the past three weeks, a year and a half after I had begun, three separate individuals have commented about a change, a visible change, they **see** in my countenance. Three weeks ago, I went to visit a friend I hadn't seen in a year and a half. A close Christian friend. After we had said our hellos and brought each other up to date on our lives, my friend said, "Anne! What has happened to you? You have never looked more beautiful! You are radiant! You are glowing!" Then about a week later, Clint and I went to a large, formal party on a Monday evening. I was not enthusiastic about going in the first place, but an old friend of the family, a gentleman, said, "What has happened to **you?** You are either pregnant or something wonderful has happened to you! You are just glowing!" This friend is not a born-again Christian. And just this morning a member of my family whom I seldom see came back to my office and said, "I have to tell you that I have never seen you looking happier! You are just glowing!" This is a dear person but not one given to glib compliments. Neither is this person even strong in expressing affirmation and warmth, nor does this person understand Christianity, but those comments were full of personal wonder and warmth.

And I have to tell you the past few months I have never felt more physically unattractive. My hair is longer than it has been in a number of years, and I am not sure I like it. I am five pounds heavier than I have been in years, and I turned 40 in 1980. (Not that that means a thing in God's kingdom!) My point is that whatever those three people saw in me, it was not in my physical appearance. It was something far deeper than that!

I truly believe what they saw in my countenance was what I have been sensing within me for months, and that is the character and nature of God being birthed within me in a way I have never known before. It had to be that glory of God shining out of me. It is only a wee beginning. It is the tender, tiny shoot that has broken forth out of the seed . . . not quite pushed through the soil yet, but birthing within me . . . deep within my spirit. Because God is infinite, there is no end to this great adventure of all adventures, just pressing on.

I feel I have only just entered into the Holy of Holies; that I have entered in to knowing Jesus, the infinite, eternal God/ man; that I have entered into Jesus **the Life.**

Where are you, my friend? Where do you want to be? Will you press on with me? For there is no end to knowing this God of ours.

PSALM 100:4: "Enter into his gates with thanksgiving **(i)**, and into his courts **(A)** with praise: be thankful unto him, and bless his name."
PSALM 100:2: "Serve the Lord with gladness; come before his presence **(C)** with singing."
PSALM 132:7-9: "We will go into his tabernacles: we will worship at his footstool. Arise, O Lord, into thy rest; thou, and the ark of thy strength. Let thy priests be clothed with righteousness; and let thy saints shout for joy."
PSALM 27:6: ". . . Therefore will I offer sacrifices of joy; I will sing, yea, I will sing praises unto the Lord."

*Heavenly Father, be with us as we pursue the greatest adventure ever lived. Still our hearts and minds. Quiet our fears as we contemplate making changes in our lives and as we consider the price we must pay for the wonder and awe of knowing You . . . really knowing You. Give us **your** strength, for we are weak and not able to press on apart from your help. Encourage us with each step we take.*

Give us a desire to live for You and You alone. Then and only then can we be fulfilled in our many roles as wives and husbands, mothers and fathers, sons and daughters, employees and employers, or whatever other roles we may serve. If we are fulfilled in You then we are fulfilled in whatever we have and do. Bless You, Lord, and thank You that we matter to You, that we are important to You. What a mighty God we serve! In Jesus' name, we pray. Amen.

Who, Not How!

EXODUS 33:13: "Now therefore, I pray thee, if I have found grace in thy sight, **shew me now thy way, that I may know thee, that I may find grace in thy sight . . .**"

Though I am in a Bible study every week and teach one each week, and know of the importance of the fellowship and feeding given and received from these meetings, I am not a person who is overly fond of seminars and books on "how to" anything. There are teachers of the Word who have imparted great truths to me and pointed me in the direction I knew I needed to go. They encouraged me and exhorted me to go on with God. They made me hungry and thirsty for Him but they seldom gave me courses in "how to" get there, at least not apart from the beauty and simplicity of the truth revealed in Scriptures. They taught me in the power of the Holy Spirit and not in the strength and wisdom of their own intellects. They stimulated me in the direction of going to God Himself to teach me, and that is what I hope to do with this book. For instance, the basic teaching in the previous chapter on the tabernacle of Moses was imparted to me by Derek Prince. It was that teaching that opened the eyes of my understanding and drew me on into the Holy of Holies. But Derek Prince didn't teach me "how." He taught me principles and spiritual truths, and God used those principles and truths to reveal to me what was missing in my life and to open up a greater dimension of truth in many areas. I was already appropriating much of what he taught, but I also saw where I needed to grow. God grew me up . . . He taught me . . . not Derek Prince. I am deeply grateful to Derek for pointing me in the right direction, but I am much more grateful to God for how He has used that teaching in my life.

I believe the Lord has given me the gift of teaching, so I am not against teachers! I am for teachers. What I am firmly against is **only** and **always** running off to Bible studies, seminars, listening to tapes and reading books as my only source for learning about the things of God. If I never go to God Himself, and to His Word, I am never sure that what I am learning from teachers is truly of God! If I don't know personally what God has to say in His Word, I have no basis for discernment. I have no plumbline for what I am being taught. There is something very lazy about a believer who will not search the Word of God for himself but prefers only to run off to hear what others believe all the time. This is how many of us are deceived into following after false doctrines.

But my primary objection to too much of this type of study, whether it be Bible study, seminars, books, tapes, etc., is that it is often majoring in the minors. The minors are fine, and we need them, but the major always should be our knowledge of and relationship with God. The Word of God says, "Seek ye first the kingdom of God and his righteousness and all these things shall be added unto thee." As we grow in the knowledge of God (Who), the minors (how) fall into place. As we become partakers of His divine nature (Who), there develops an understanding of the spirit of the Law rather than majoring in the letter of the Law (how). And I believe a result of that is that faith grows into a knowledge of God that is as unshakable as $2 + 2 = 4$. We grow from faith in Jesus as The Way to salvation to knowledge of Jesus as The Way to Truth and to The Life in the kingdom of God. I know a few Christians who have known the Lord as "The Life" in the Holy of Holies for thirty to forty years, and it is visibly obvious. You cannot miss it. And that sparks me to a healthy jealousy. It is "salt" that makes me thirsty. It sparks me to press on.

My greatest hope about this book is that it will help do the

same for you, that it will make you hungry and thirsty for God
. to press on to the mark for the prize of the high calling of
God in Christ Jesus . . . to know Him, to search out His Word,
to love and adore Him, to enter into praise and worship of
Him. For He is worthy of that from each one of us. He is
worthy of our giving Him all that we have within us.

He is not only worthy, but His very character and presence
evoke praise and worship deep within us. It is the rivers of
living waters that overflow from the heart of every worshiper in
spirit and in truth. He is the source of all praise and worship.
He is the Who who will bring it to pass. It is in the knowing of
Him that praise and worship spring forth. If we do not draw
near to God, if we do not give Him the private, personal time of
praise and adoration and prayer that He so richly deserves and
intensely desires from us, we have nothing to respond to.

We praise in the beginning "by faith," in obedience to His
many commands. He then responds to our praises.

PSALM 22:3: "But thou art holy, O thou **that inhabitest the
praises of Israel.**"

There are many places God demonstrates this truth in
scripture. Let's look at one.

2 CHRONICLES 5:12–14: "(. . . Also the Levites which were the
singers, all of them of Asaph, of Heman, of Jeduthun, with
their sons and their brethren, being arrayed in white linen,
having cymbals and psalteries and harps, stood at the east end
of the altar, and with them an hundred and twenty priests
sounding with trumpets:) It came even to pass, as the trumpe-
ters and singers were as one, to make one sound to be heard in
praising and thanking the Lord; and when they lifted up their
voice with the trumpets and cymbals and instruments of music,
and praised the Lord, saying, For he is good; for his mercy
endureth for ever: that **then** the house was filled with a cloud,
even the house of the Lord; So that the priests could not stand
to minister by reason of the cloud: for **the glory of the Lord had
filled the house of God.**"

As God responds to praise by falling in our midst, our next

response is worship, which involves our bodies. Every word for worship in the Hebrew pertains to a bodily posture . . . kneeling, bowing, prostrating oneself, lifting of hands, etc. It is here in the midst of worship, in the midst of His glory, that He reveals Himself. It is in this revelation, fellowship, communion and worship that our relationship with Him develops.

Trust God (Who) to show you how in **His** Word first. Remember His Word is our plumbline. Then you can trust Him to lead you into the reality of it in your personal life.

I am reminded of Psalm 119 where the Psalmist continuously praises the Lord and beseeches the Lord's wisdom and instruction. "How sweet are thy words unto my taste! yea, sweeter than honey to my mouth! . . . I have not departed from thy judgments: for thou hast taught me. . . . Through thy precepts I get understanding: therefore I hate every false way. . . . Oh how I love thy law! it is my meditation all the day. . . . Stablish thy word unto thy servant, who is devoted to thy fear. . . . Teach me good judgment and knowledge: for I have believed thy commandments. . . . Thy word is a lamp unto my feet, and a light unto my path. . . . Let my cry come near before thee, O Lord: give me understanding according to thy word. . . . The entrance of thy words giveth light; it giveth understanding unto the simple. . . . I have more understanding than all my teachers: for thy testimonies are my meditation." (vv. 103, 102, 104, 97, 38, 66, 105, 169, 130, 99.) God and His Word can be trusted! He will not lead you astray.

Our church doctrines will pass away. In times of persecution of the Church, our doctrines are not what sustain us. Around the world today, the Church of Jesus Christ is suffering horrendous persecution. Christians are being attacked and abused verbally and physically by governments and peoples. And through it all it has not been denominational doctrine that has enabled them to persevere, to "endure until the end," but rather it is the relationship of the individual believer to God that sustains him and gives comfort to others in those times. It is a depth of relationship, profound and abiding in the knowledge of the Holy Lord God Almighty. I repeat, that relationship is built in praise and worship. So let's press on to see what, or at least part of what, God has to say on the subject. Let's ask Who to teach us how!

ISAIAH 64:4, 7: "For since the beginning of the world men have not heard, nor perceived by the ear, neither hath the eye seen, O God, beside thee, what he hath prepared for him that waiteth for him. . . . (but) there is none that calleth upon thy name, that stirreth up himself to take hold of thee: for thou hast hid thy face from us, and hast consumed us, because of our iniquities."

Shall we stir ourselves up? As we now move on to the heart of this book, let us take the words of Paul and keep them ever before us, "Brethren, I count not myself to have apprehended: but this one thing I do, forgetting those things which are behind, and reaching forth unto those things which are before, I press toward the mark for the prize of the high calling of God in Christ Jesus" (Phil. 3:13–14).

2 CORINTHIANS 4:6: "For God . . . hath shined in our hearts, to give the **light** of the knowledge of the glory of God in the face of Jesus Christ."

Lord! God! Father! We come before You right now, confessing that we are not able of ourselves to do what You have called us to do. We are unable to be what You want us to be. We call upon You, our Creator. We stir ourselves up to take hold of You. We call upon the mighty and matchless name of Jesus to open our eyes, to soften our hearts, to enable us to know the breadth, and length, and depth, and height of the exceeding greatness and unsearchable riches of Your love, which passes knowledge, that we might be filled with all of the fullness of God. You who are able to do exceeding abundantly above all that we ask or think, according to the power that works within us, to You be the glory. In Jesus' name. Amen.

The Heart of the Matter

In Earth As It Is in Heaven

ACTS 24:14: "... I confess unto thee that, after the way which they call heresy, so worship I the God of my fathers, believing all things which are written in the law and in the prophets."

In Earth
As It Is in Heaven

As the Lord began to draw me into Davidic praise and worship,* I began to study and meditate upon the subject in God's Word. One day as I was driving down the street listening to the radio, someone began to teach on the Lord's prayer, and the words, "Thy kingdom come. Thy will be done in earth, as it is in heaven," dropped into my heart. We learned in the tabernacle teaching that that is called Rhema. It is revelation from God. And this was clearly revelation from God to me. It was God saying to me, "My daughter, listen to these words. Do you understand them?" I knew then that the Lord was giving me an important key to His kingdom, right there in my car, as I was driving down Preston Road in Dallas, Texas.

Suddenly all of those verses in Revelation began to flood my heart as I saw in the spirit the four living creatures and the four and twenty elders, and all of the hosts of heaven praising and worshiping God extravagantly and passionately.

It was this revelation from the Lord that gave birth to the book you are reading. It is the key to understanding Davidic praise and worship and its relevance in your life and mine, for I earnestly believe it is the desire of God's heart today that all of His children enter into the ministry of Davidic praise and

*My term used throughout this book in reference to the praise of the Psalms and much of the Old Testament and the Book of the Revelation.

worship. David did. The apostles did. And all over the world today, the church of Jesus Christ is being drawn to adore God in this way. And the Lord wants to continue to reach out and touch people who have not heard nor understood or do not know. And I believe that He has called me to write this book as a part of His reaching out to draw us to Himself. I ardently pray that it will open the eyes of your understanding as it has mine.

For a clear understanding of exactly what God means by praise and worship, let's look first into the Book of Revelation and then into a few of the many references elsewhere. Then we will look at what Jesus had to say on the subject. Please read them carefully. Allow yourself to be caught up in John's vision.

REVELATION 4:6–11: "And before the throne there was a sea of glass like crystal: and in the midst of the throne, and round about the throne, were four beasts full of eyes before and behind. And the first beast was like a lion, and the second beast like a calf, and the third beast had a face as a man, and the fourth beast was like a flying eagle. And the four beasts had each of them six wings about him; and they were full of eyes within: and **they rest not day and night,** saying, Holy, holy, holy, Lord God Almighty, which was, and is, and is to come. And when those beasts give glory and honor and thanks to him that sat on the throne, who liveth for ever and ever, The four and twenty elders fall down before him that sat on the throne, and worship him that liveth for ever and ever, and cast their crowns before the throne, saying, Thou art worthy, O Lord, to receive glory and honor and power; for thou hast created all things, and for thy pleasure they are and were created."

REVELATION 5:8–14: "And when he had taken the book, the four beasts and four and twenty elders fell down before the Lamb, having every one of them harps, and golden vials full of odours, which are the prayers of the saints. And they sung a new song, saying, Thou art worthy to take the book, and to open the seals thereof: for thou wast slain, and hast redeemed us to God by thy blood out of every kindred, and tongue, and people, and nation; And hast made us unto our God kings and priests: and we shall reign on the earth. And I beheld, and I heard the voice of many angels round about the throne and the beasts and the elders: and the number of them was ten thousand times ten thousand, and thousands of thousands; Saying with a loud voice, Worthy is the Lamb that was slain to receive power, and riches, and wisdom, and strength, and honour, and glory, and blessing. And every creature which is in heaven, and on the earth and under the earth, and such as are in the sea, and all that are in them, heard I saying, Blessing, and honour, and glory, and power, be unto him that sitteth upon the throne, and unto the Lamb, for ever and ever. And the four said, Amen. And the four and twenty elders fell down and worshipped him that liveth for ever and ever."

REVELATION 7:9–12: "After this I beheld, and, lo, a great multitude, which no man could number, of all nations, and kindreds, and people, and tongues, stood before the throne, and before the Lamb, clothed with white robes, and palms in their hands; And cried with a loud voice, saying, Salvation to our God which sitteth upon the throne, and unto the Lamb. And all the angels stood round about the throne, and about the elders and the four beasts, and fell before the throne on their faces, and worshipped God, Saying, Amen: Blessing, and glory, and wisdom, and thanksgiving, and honour, and power, and might, be unto our God for ever and ever. Amen."

REVELATION 11:15–17: "And the seventh angel sounded; and there were great voices in heaven, saying, The kingdoms of this world are become the kingdoms of our Lord, and of his Christ; and he shall reign for ever and ever. And the four and twenty elders, which sat before God on their seats, fell upon their faces, and worshipped God, Saying, We give thee thanks, O Lord God Almighty, which art, and wast, and art to come; because thou hast taken to thee thy great power, and hast reigned."

REVELATION 19:1–7: "And after these things I heard a great voice of many people in heaven, saying, Alleluia; Salvation, and glory, and honour, and power, unto the Lord, our God: For true and righteous are his judgments: for he hath judged the great whore, which did corrupt the earth with her fornication, and hath avenged the blood of his servants at her hand. And again, they said, Alleluia. And her smoke rose up for ever and ever. And the four and twenty elders and the four beasts fell down and worshipped God that sat on the throne, saying, Amen; Alleluia! And a voice came out of the throne, saying, Praise our God, all ye his servants, and ye that fear him, both small and great. And I heard as it were the voice of a great multitude, and as the voice of many waters, and as the voice of mighty thunderings, saying, Alleluia: for the Lord God omnipotent reigneth. Let us be glad and rejoice, and give honour to him: for the marriage of the Lamb is come, and his wife hath made herself ready."

It sounds as if heaven is a very "noisy" place to me. Just a cursory glance through the Book of Revelation reveals verse after verse of references to all kinds of "beings" speaking forth in a "loud voice, sounding (forth as a trumpet; a loud blast), the voice of great multitudes and as the sound of many waters and as the sound of mighty thunderings, etc." In fact, in all of eternity there is apparently only thirty minutes of silence, and that is so unusual that the Bible even mentions it (Rev. 8:1).

Noise is generally not associated with things of God, but rather it is associated with things of the world, both pleasant and unpleasant. Yet the Bible very definitely states over and over again that heaven is noisy and overtly passionate in its demonstration of praise and worship to God. And all through the Bible we see great evidence that the saints understood they were created for this purpose and participated in this joyful noise.

1 PETER 2:9: "But ye are a chosen generation, a royal priesthood, an holy nation, a peculiar people; that ye should shew forth the praises of him who hath called you out of darkness into his marvelous light."
HEBREWS 13:15: "By him therefore let us offer the sacrifice of praise to God continually, that is, the fruit of our lips giving thanks to his name."
ISAIAH 43:21: "This people have I formed for myself; they shall shew forth my praise."
PSALM 148:14: "He also exalteth the horn of his people, the praise of all his saints. . . .
ISAIAH 61:11: ". . . the Lord God will cause righteousness and praise to spring forth before all nations."

PSALM 98:4,6: "Make a joyful noise unto the Lord, all the earth: make a loud noise, and rejoice, and sing praise. . . . With trumpets and sound of cornet make a joyful noise before the Lord, the King."

PSALM 35:27: "Let them shout for joy, and be glad, that favor my righteous cause: yea, let them say continually, Let the Lord be magnified, which hath pleasure in the prosperity of his servant."

ISAIAH 42:11: ". . . let the inhabitants of the rock sing, let them shout from the top of the mountains."

2 SAMUEL 6:14: "And David danced before the Lord with all his might; . . ."

PSALM 134:2: "Lift up your hands in the sanctuary, and bless the Lord."

LUKE 24:50–53: "And he (Jesus) led them out as far as to Bethany, and he lifted up his hands, and blessed them. And it came to pass, while he blessed them, he was parted from them, and carried up into heaven. And they worshipped (fell on their faces before) him, and returned to Jerusalem with great joy: And were continually in the temple, praising and blessing God. Amen."

Isaiah, David, Peter, Paul were all Jews. They were already praisers and worshipers. The Bible is full to overflowing with this extravagant, demonstrative, passionate, active praise. It is Jewish. We are spiritual Jews. Jesus was a Jew. He had much to say, if not in quantity, in quality, on this subject of praise and worship.

"But the hour cometh, and now is, when the true worshippers shall worship the Father in spirit and in truth: for the Father seeketh such to worship him. God is a spirit: and they that worship him must worship him in spirit and in truth" (John 4:23–24). The Greek word here for "worship" is *proßkuněō*, and it means "to prostrate oneself in homage (to do reverence to; adore): worship." The same word is used in Matthew 2:11, Luke 24:52, in all instances in Revelation, and in many other places in the New Testament. In some instances it appears translated into English as "worship" and in others it appears as "fell on their faces."

When the Pharisees ordered Jesus to rebuke the multitudes

for rejoicing and praising God with a loud voice for all the mighty works that they had seen Jesus perform, He answered them, ". . . I tell you that, if these should hold their peace, the stones would immediately cry out" (Luke 19:40). And when the chief priests and scribes saw the children crying out and praising God in the temple and told Jesus to silence them, Jesus said, ". . . Have ye never read, Out of the mouth of babes and sucklings thou has perfected praise?" (Matt. 21:16). In Luke 6:23, He said to the multitudes, "Rejoice ye in that day, and leap for joy. . . ." The Greek word for "leap for joy" here is *skirtaō*, and "leap for joy" is the literal translation.

We don't have a lot of scriptural references to Jesus' personal devotional life, but what we do know about Him reveals that He was a very passionate and demonstrative man. There is one reference that clearly reveals that quality in Jesus' prayer life. "In that hour he (Jesus) rejoiced in the Holy Spirit, and said, I thank thee, Father, Lord of heaven and earth, that thou hast hidden these things from the wise and understanding and revealed them to babes: yea, Father, for such was thy gracious will" (Luke 10:21, RSV). The Greek word for "rejoiced" used in this reference is *agalliaō*, and it translates, "to jump for joy, i.e., exult." Jesus jumped for joy in the Holy Spirit and praised God.

And there is a reference in Hebrews which quotes Jesus as saying, "I will declare thy name unto my brethren, in the midst of the church will I sing praise unto thee" (2:12). This verse is a direct quote from Psalm 22 which speaks prophetically of Jesus' crucifixion and resurrection. "I will declare thy name unto my brethren: in the midst of the congregation will I praise thee" (v. 22). We will be studying the Hebrew root words for praise in the chapter entitled "Finding Lost Treasure," but for now I will briefly tell you that the Hebrew word for praise used in Psalm 22:22 is *hâlal*, which means "to celebrate, make a show of, boast, rave." This word for "praise" connotes extravagance in demonstration.

Quoting Andrew Murray in *God's Best Secrets*, "The angels are ever abiding flames of pure love, always ascending up to and uniting with God, because the glory, the love, and goodness of God alone, is all that they see and know, either within or without themselves. The adoration in spirit and in truth never ceases, because they never cease to acknowledge the all of God in themselves, and the all of God in the whole creation. This is the one religion of heaven, and nothing else is the truth of religion on earth."

As temples of the Holy Spirit of God, as members of the precious body of Jesus Christ, as people walking around with Jesus **in** us, should our response be any less than that of the angels? **No!** I believe that praise and worship are what Jesus meant when He said, "Thy kingdom come. Thy will be done, **in earth as it is in heaven."**

And here I would like to make a critical link in the Rhema I received driving down the road in my car that day and Rhema I received months later regarding those words. It came after I had added the tabernacle teaching to this book, which did not come until the final rewrite of the manuscript. So you see, God has continued to unfold His truth to me on this subject. The book could not go to print because He had not finished teaching me what He wanted me to teach you.

Here it is. Praise and worship **in earth as it is in heaven** (at the altar of incense) are the link between the spirit-filled, spirit-led believer and the Presence of God and His kingdom-life **in earth as it is in heaven** (in the Holy of Holies). "Thy kingdom come. Thy will be done, **in earth as it is in heaven."** Praise and worship are one of the missing keys to the kingdom. And He is putting those keys back into our hands today.

Jesus originally gave the keys to the kingdom to Peter (Matt. 16:19), but you know how easy it is to lose keys, don't you! And we will study in a later chapter how the keys got lost, but there is one more piece of the puzzle I would like to slip into place. In fact, I think it is another one of the missing keys.

MATTHEW 18:3–4: "And (Jesus) said, Verily I say unto you, Except ye be converted, and **(then) become as little children** (after conversion!), **ye shall not enter into the kingdom of heaven** (the Holy of Holies). Whosoever therefore shall humble himself as this little child, the same is greatest in the kingdom of heaven."

MARK 10:14–15: ". . . Suffer the little children to come unto me, and forbid them not: for **of such is the kingdom of God.** Verily

I say unto you, **Whosoever shall not receive the kingdom of God as a little child, he shall not enter therein."**

The writer to the Hebrews said it is impossible to please God without faith. Jesus said it is impossible to enter into the kingdom of God without childlike faith. And there is a strong connection between Davidic praise and worship and childlike faith. It isn't "sophisticated." It isn't even what many would consider "proper." It is childlike. It is open, free, expressive and it is offered up to God with all that is within us.

Children are basically uninhibited and open before loving parents, and I believe that these attitudes of childlike playfulness are especially essential to understanding the spiritual truths of praise and worship before our heavenly Father. Have you ever watched little children play? They wrestle, they run, they laugh, they yell. Whatever children do that they enjoy, they do it with abandon. They do it with all that is within them. David very obviously had the heart of a child, and Scripture says he had a heart after God.

Let's look at a few of those references. 2 Samuel 6:14 says, "And David danced before the Lord with all his might; . . ." The Hebrew word for danced is *kârar* and it means "to dance (i.e., whirl)." And please notice that David danced with all his **might.** We will study this word *might* a little later in the book, but for now let me just tell you that it means "power, strength, boldness, might, praise." Second Samuel 6:16 tells us that King David was "leaping and dancing before the Lord." The Hebrew word for leaping is *pâzaz*, and it means "to solidify (as if by refining); also to spring (as if separating the limbs):—leap, be made strong." It is interesting that *Strong's* says it also means "to refine (gold):—best (gold)." In 2 Samuel 6:21 David responded to the scornful attitude of Michal to his behavior by saying, "Therefore will I play before the Lord." The Hebrew word used here for "play" is *sâchaq*, which is defined as "to laugh (in pleasure), by implication, to play: make merry, rejoice, laugh." And once again in 1 Chronicles 15:29 we see King David "dancing and playing" before the Ark of the Covenant of the Lord. The Hebrew word used here for dancing is *râqad*. This word means "to stamp, i.e., to spring about (wildly or for joy):—dance, jump, leap, skip."

This childlike faith and freedom of expression is another key to the kingdom, and it is certainly the key to entering into Davidic praise and worship.

Since there is so much meat in this chapter, I think it would be a good idea to recap the truths we have studied. (1) There is a clear connection between heavenly praise and worship and Davidic praise and worship. (2) Praise and worship are active, enthusiastic, passionate and demonstrative, and not passive. (3) It is God's will for all his children. (4) Childlike faith is essential to growing into all truth, especially in relation to this book, praise and worship, and the kingdom of God. (5) Praise and worship are eternal. They were, are, and always will be.

PSALM 111:10: ". . . his praise endureth for ever."

PSALM 145:2: ". . . I will praise thy name for ever and ever."

PSALM 45:17: "I will make thy name to be remembered in all generations: therefore shall the people praise thee for ever and ever."

REVELATION 7:15: "Therefore are they before the throne of God, and serve (worship) him day and night in his temple: and he that sitteth on the throne shall dwell among them."

Dear Lord, as the hart pants after the water brooks, so my soul longs for You, O God. My soul thirsts for You, the living God, in a dry and thirsty land. I lift my hands to You in surrender. As a little child comes to his daddy, I come to You, raising my hands to be lifted up to your bosom, to be held closely to your own heart. Give me a heart like David's, Lord. Give me a heart that is after You, to fulfill all your will. Give me a childlike quality and ability to praise and worship You, that I might draw near to Your Presence. You said, "Ask and ye shall receive. Draw near to me and I will draw near unto you." We ask, dear Lord. We draw near. And it is in Your name and for Your sake that we pray. Amen.

With Vehemence?

DEUTERONOMY 6:4–5: "Hear, O Israel: The Lord our God is one Lord: And thou shalt love the Lord thy God with **all** thine heart, and with **all** thy soul, and with **all** thy might."

PSALM 111:1: "Praise ye the Lord. I will praise the Lord **with my whole heart,** in the assembly of the upright, and in the congregation."

I am most grateful to the Lord for leading me to a church that praises and worships the way the Bible tells us David did and the heavenly hosts do. It has borne much fruit in my life, a greater harvest of fruit—"love, joy, peace, long-suffering, gentleness, goodness, faith, meekness and temperance." But the greatest blessing I've experienced from this ministry to God is the growing depth and profundity of my relationship with the Living God, into a heartthrobbing intimacy and love beyond my greatest hopes. And I look forward to a continuation of that growth and development throughout eternity.

Among many people today there is no understanding of Davidic praise and worship, and it is looked upon with disdain and with an attitude that it is overemotionalism. As one who participates in this type of praise and worship toward God every Sunday and in my personal, daily devotional life, I can truthfully say that it is not overemotionalism. I do not believe we can be overemotional in our response to the Lord. Rather, it is a premeditated and purposeful act toward God in obedience to an eternal spiritual law. It doesn't just happen. Many

Sundays I go to church not "feeling" at all like praising God, but, first, I don't go by "feelings," and, second, I can tell you that I look forward to it with great anticipation, no matter how I "feel."

I praise God because He is God, and He is worthy to be praised! Whether I feel like it or not! In fact, some of the greatest praise that has poured forth from my heart to God's has come on the days when I "felt" the lowest!

I am sure that Paul and Silas didn't "feel" like praising God when they were stripped of their clothes, beaten, thrown into prison with their feet "fast in the stocks." Scripture says that they prayed and sang praises unto God. The result of their outpouring to God was mighty signs and wonders in their midst, resulting in their deliverance from bondage and the salvation of the jailer and his family (Acts 16:22–34). What would have happened if they had given in to their "feelings" and moaned and groaned about their situation? What if they had gone to sleep from exhaustion? Paul and Silas most definitely did not wait to praise God until they "felt" like it. In obedience to the commands of God, they prayed and praised in spirit and in truth.

The most commonly used Hebrew word for praise is *hâlal.* Expanding on the use referred to earlier, *Strong's* tells us it means "to shine; hence, to make a show, to boast; and thus to be (clamorously) foolish; to rave; to celebrate." Overemotional? Or is it merely giving the Lord all that He desires and deserves? Is not the heart the seat of the emotions? And are we not to love Him with all of it?

DEUTERONOMY 6:5: "And thou shalt love the Lord thy God with all thine heart, and with all thy soul, and with all thy might."

The Hebrew word for "might" is $m^{e,}od$, which translates, "vehemence; wholly; utterly." *Vehemence* is defined in *Webster's Collegiate Dictionary* as "marked by exertion of great force or energy; marked by strong feeling; forcible expression; passionate; intense."

God has commanded us to love Him with all our hearts, souls and might. That is with great force and energy, with strong feeling, with forcible expression. Passionately. Intensely. With all that is within us.

Before we leave this teaching, I would like to take a look at the word *dignity*, as used earlier in the definition for *glory* , with reference to the cherubim of "glory" over the mercy seat in the Holy of Holies. (See Heb. 9:5.) Because of my cultural background, my understanding of that word did not fit with what I know to be the biblical perspective on praise and worship. Rather than trust my instincts about the meaning of this word, I went first to the 1828 facsimile edition of *Webster's Dictionary*. Here is what it said: "to be good, to avail, to be worth, to be profitable. True honor; nobleness or elevation of mind, consisting in a high sense of propriety, truth and justice, with an abhorrence of mean and sinful actions; opposed to meanness." I then went to my 1964 *Webster's New World Dictionary of the American Language* to see how it defined *dignity*, because the 1828 edition did not fully represent to me my perception of the meaning of the word and I wanted to know if my perception was invalid. To my amazement I saw clearly what our culture has done to our way of seeing things. In addition to the above definitions, there were two very interesting additional definitions: (1) loftiness, haughtiness of appearance or manner; stateliness; and (2) calm SELF-possession and SELF-respect." The synonym given is *decorum*. Looking that word up, it said, "whatever is suitable or proper; propriety and good taste in behavior, speech, dress, etc.; implies stiffness or formality in rules of conduct or behavior **established** as suitable to the circumstances." Now *that* was my perception of the word *dignity!* And yet I was puzzled about how we could have gotten so far off the track from the early roots of the word . . . how we came from "true honor, truth, justice and propriety" to "stiffness or formality in rules of conduct or behavior." I then went to the Hebrew to see what the original intent of the word was. In Hebrew the word is *s⁰eth*, and it means "elevation; figuratively, ELATION OR CHEERFULNESS; exaltation in rank or character: be accepted, dignity, excellency, highness, raise up self, rising." I find it fascinating that elation and cheerfulness are correlated to dignity, excellency, and highness. What a tragedy that these important elements of truth have been lost to our sophisticated society over these past centuries and we have consequently lost an important key to the kingdom of God. Therefore we are missing an important element of our faith and spiritual lives, and that is a childlikeness. As I wrote in the introduction to this book, God does not love us commensurate with our good works, including Davidic praise and worship. However, Davidic praise and worship are important avenues through which the love of God can flow from Him to us.

In addition, my own personal perceptions of God have begun to change as I have pored over the Word of God. My mental image of God fit with my contemporary (and erroneous) image of the word *dignity*. I saw God as somber, sober-faced, staid, stiff, formal . . . and dignified. And those descriptions may also fit Him at times. I don't know. What I do know is that they do not **always** fit Him. He is omnipotent, He is glorious and majestic. He is stately. He is power, He is wisdom, He is eternal God and there is no one like Him. He is all-knowing. He is holy and mighty. He is too wonderful for words. He is delightful. He is wrath. He is justice. He is love. He is mercy and tender loving kindness. He is all this and more. Much, much more. And He Who calls His people to praise and worship Him with vehemence, with all that is within us, body, soul and spirit; He Who created us in His image, He Who gave us our emotions to praise and honor and glorify Him, demonstrates that He too is a God of great emotion. His Bible is full, page after page, of His emotion . . . the outpouring of His love, mercy, wrath, etc. He is fiercely and passionately emotional.

One Sunday morning in our church, after we had praised and worshiped vehemently, a woman came forward and said that she had seen God in a vision. He was above the sanctuary, and He was rejoicing over the congregation with great joy. She said He was spinning around and leaping and laughing and rejoicing over us in response to our sacrifice of praise and worship to Him. The woman was deeply, deeply touched by what she saw. As she left the microphone, one of our pastors came and read the following scripture, confirming what she saw.

ZEPHANIAH 3:17: "The Lord thy God in the midst of thee is

mighty; he will save, he will rejoice over thee with joy; he will rest in his love, he will joy over thee with singing."

A lovely verse in the King James translation, isn't it? But if we look deeper into the Hebrew we get great insight into a side of God of which most of us have no perception.

English	Hebrew	Translation
mighty	*gibbôr*	powerful; warrior; mighty one
save	*yâsha'*	to be (or set) free; to deliver; to avenge
rejoice	*sîys*	to be bright; to radiate; to be joyful
joy (1)	*simchâh*	glee; exceeding gladness
rest	*chârash*	to be silent (I would interpret this as experiencing a love too great for words)
joy (2)	*gûwl*	to spin around (under the influence of any violent emotion) in rejoicing
singing	*rinnâh*	triumphant shouts of joy

Please note before we go further that I have used the applications and definitions that fit the context of the scripture. There are other definitions under some of the words . . . and other applications. If you would like to check them out for yourself, I used the Hebrew and Greek dictionaries contained in the *Strong's Exhaustive Concordance of the Bible*. It would be a wonderful thing if you would search out the scriptures for yourself. Don't just take my word for it. Don't be content to let me do your thinking for you.

Now that we have looked at the English and Hebrew words and studied their translations, let me give you Anne Murchison's interpretation of Zephaniah 3:17: "The Lord thy God, in the midst of thee is a mighty warrior; he will save and deliver thee, he will shine forth over thee with great glee, he will be silent in his great love for thee, he will spin around in violent emotion over thee with triumphant shouts of great joy!"

There is quite a range of emotions reflected in the above verse when we study the words in their original meaning and intent. The Lord our God is a God of great emotion and feeling and His people are created in His image. May those emotions bring us joy and ease our fears. May they become a reality in our lives that more and more of God will become a reality to us!

Does that sound radical to you? Well, I'll tell you what I think. God is extremely radical. The Bible is exceptionally radical. Jesus was a radical. His disciples were radicals. And I am being conformed to His image.

Overemotional? Let me tell you what overemotional is. Before I was a Christian and for quite a time after my commitment, I was a very overemotional person. My husband says I was vitriolic. A friend says I was petulant. I cried every day, and not just cried, but wept and wailed bitterly, sobbing for hours. I screamed at the top of my lungs in frustration. I cursed. I kicked. I threw things. I hit people. That, my friend, is overemotional! And yet since I have begun to give my emotions to the Lord in the scriptural method of Davidic praise and worship, my depression, frustration, and outbursts are gone. I believe our emotions were created for the Lord, and they find sweet release when they are offered up to Him. Love, adoration, praise and worship are all matters which issue forth from our hearts. They are emotional responses.

Overemotionalism connotes someone or something out of control. And there are those of us who actually are not under the control of the Holy Spirit but **are** out of control. There are those of us who have not come to the table of shewbread and allowed the Lord to bring our wills under His control. There are those of us who praise according to the flesh (the Adamic ego . . . the carnal, unrenewed mind), and not according to the spirit.

Before I began to study the scriptures on Davidic praise and worship, what I saw of it all looked like overemotionalism to me! I'll never forget the first time I saw a group of the Lord's people on television praising Him in this way. I felt embarrassed. But I know now that that was my problem, not theirs. It was my lack of spiritual understanding and insight. In my study of the word, I believe the Lord has given me His light on the subject. He has revealed His desire to me, and I believe He has called me to share it. We have overlooked these truths for a long time, but God is beginning to shed much light on them to many persons all over the world. And how, you may be wondering, do I know it is light? These verses are my plumbline.

JAMES 3:14–18: "But if ye have bitter envying and strife in your hearts, glory not, and lie not against the truth. This wisdom descendeth not from above, but is earthly, sensual, devilish. For where envying and strife is, there is confusion and every evil work. But the wisdom that is from above is first pure, then peaceable, gentle, and easy to be entreated, full of mercy and good fruits, without partiality, and without hypocrisy. And the fruit of righteousness is sown in peace by them that make peace."

GALATIANS 5:22–23: "But the fruit of the Spirit is love, joy, peace, longsuffering, gentleness, goodness, faith, Meekness, temperance: against such there is no law."

God's wisdom brings peace and the fruit of righteousness. And that is how a believer can know he or she is walking in the light. It is true that Satan can appear as an angel of light, but the fruit of his wisdom is earthly (worldly), sensual and/or demoniacal. He brings bitter envyings and strife into the heart of a believer. So if you have ever wondered how to tell the difference, Scripture has given us a means of discerning the validity of what we perceive as truth in our lives.

In fact, speaking of the devil, it's very interesting to see how Satan has robbed the body of Christ of its most important ministry. But, of course, who would know better than Satan where to hit us where it would hurt the most? Scripture reveals that he was, before his exile, God's anointed cherub, and that he was the chief musician in charge of praise in heaven. ". . . the workmanship of thy tabrets (tambourines) and of thy pipes was prepared in thee in the day that thou wast created. Thou art the anointed cherub that covereth; and I have set thee so. . . ." (Ezek. 28:13–14). (Remember the cherubim which cover the mercy seat in the Holy of Holies?)

Is it any surprise then that, as the former anointed covering cherub of God (that is, one of the cherubim over the heavenly Ark of the Covenant), Satan would set his own priorities to destroy this ministry to the Creator in the only place that he has any authority, that is, here on earth? He has not only managed to blind the eyes of Christians to this wonderful truth, but he has succeeded in perverting music from praise to God to praise to himself in the world. He has taken what was pure and lovely and virtuous out of the realm of God's people and placed it in the hands of his own followers, the lost people of the world. All hard rock—and, I sincerely believe, all rock—is the ultimate in degradation and perversion of the "original" music and is totally dedicated to the destruction of the world through the devastation of our young people. It speaks often in terms of worship to the chief pervert himself, Satan, and of every sick, perverse thing that is going on in the world today.

Have you ever seen the connection between rock music and those bombed-out, bleary-eyed, drug-abused, purposeless, promiscuous teenagers of the last fifteen or twenty years? There definitely is a connection. And so much of the remainder of secular, contemporary pop music, and I include country and western in this category, speaks of the futility, hopelessness and frustration of living in a fallen world. But the one form of music ordained by God, the extravagant Davidic praise and worship toward God, is uncomfortable for many of us. But the truth of God is beautiful to the hungry-hearted Christian. Let us continue to press on to the mark of the prize of the high calling of God in Christ Jesus. God is restoring Davidic praise and worship to His church. Greater is He that is in us than he that is in the world!

PSALM 103:1: "Bless the Lord, O my soul: and **all** that is within me, bless his holy name."
MARK 12:29–30: "And Jesus answered him, The first of all the commandments is, Hear, O Israel; The Lord our God is one Lord: And thou shalt love the Lord thy God with **all** thy heart, and with **all** thy soul, and with **all** thy mind, and with **all** thy strength: this is the first commandment."

Lord God Almighty! We have long honored You with our lips but our hearts have been far from You. In vain do we worship You and teach as doctrines the commandments of men. We have lain aside the commandments of God and held to the tradition of men. Full well we have rejected the commandment of God, that we may keep our own traditions. Forgive us and enable us to see the truth. Enable us to cast down imaginations and every high thing that exalts itself against the knowledge of You. Enable us by your Spirit to bring into captivity every thought to the obedience of Jesus Christ. Not by might, not by power, but by your Spirit, Lord. Cause our blind eyes to see, our dumb mouths to speak and sing praises to You. Cause our limp arms to reach up to You, our heavenly Father. Cause our feet to rejoice and leap for joy. Cause our hearts to open up to receive the wonderful love of God, the honey from the rock. We want to know You, Lord. We want to please You. Cause your life and Godly emotions to flow through us to You. Make of us worshipers in spirit and in truth. In the mighty name of Jesus. Amen.

Lost—a Set of Keys

As I continued to read and study on this wonderful and vast subject of Davidic praise and worship, I kept asking, "What happened? Why did the church stop doing it? If it is so important to the Lord and to the believer too, how could we have lost sight of it as such an important key to the kingdom?"

I remember reading in two places in my studies that the church lost its life and power during the Dark or Middle Ages. No one knows exactly what moment, day or month, or even year that life stopped, but a concensus among many who have studied this subject is that it occurred early in the beginning of this dark period in history.

Webster's New World Dictionary defines this period in history as beginning at the fall of the Western Roman Empire (A.D. 476) and ending at the start of the modern era (A.D. 1450). The terms "middle" or "dark" ages arose from the idea that the medieval period in Europe, especially the earlier part, was characterized by widespread ignorance, lack of progress, etc. *Noah Webster's First Edition of an American Dictionary of the English Language* (facsimile edition), defines this period in history as the ages or period of time about equally distant from the decline of the Roman Empire and the revival of letters in Europe, or from the eighth to the fifteenth century of the Christian era.

It is generally agreed that this was not only a time of ignorance and darkness intellectually, culturally, sociologically, and scientifically, but it was a very dark time for the church spiritually. It was the time of the Crusades in the Middle East and the Spanish Inquisitions. It was a time of brutality and tyranny as Christianity was forced upon the people for the selfish political purposes of despotic oppressors. Those resisting or refusing were persecuted and condemned. It was a bleak and bloody period in human history.

Add to that the fact that because ignorance and illiteracy prevailed, the common man had no access to the written word of any kind, but for purposes of our study, it is significant that only a very few had access to the Word of God. You can well understand that the church fell into almost total darkness. I say almost, because the Lord always has His remnant of believers. History reveals that there were during this period spirit-filled believers, but only a mere handful. For the most part, the church of Jesus Christ lost its life's blood. It ceased to be a faith in the Living God and became the state religion, forced upon even the most unwilling.

Not only did the people not have the Word of God for the renewing of their minds, but the wisdom of man replaced the wisdom of God as men interpreted the Word as they pleased. Many of the Lord's truths were perverted or supplanted with man's rules and regulations, and the church became ritualistic and dead rather than flowing in truth and spirit. In my opinion, and in the opinion of many Bible scholars, the judgment of God fell upon the church. It happened to the Israelites. And it happened to the New Testament church. Amos prophesied about this.

AMOS 8:11–12: "Behold, the days come, saith the Lord God, that I will send a famine in the land, not a famine of bread, nor a thirst for water, but of hearing the words of the Lord: And they shall wander . . . to and fro to seek the word of the Lord, and shall not find it."

But the Lord had plans for the world that could not be thwarted. He began to lift His hand of judgment from us and out of this vast abyss of darkness He began to turn the lights back on. Not all at once, but, rather, one by one He returned the keys to the kingdom to us. Luther, Calvin, the Wesleys, Edwards, Moody, Finney, Sunday, and a host of others all played a part in the restoration of the church of Jesus Christ. And the Lord is *still* turning on lights. Almost every key is back in place, though the news may not have reached some portions of the church yet. And every time a new light twinkles on, every time a key is returned, there is stiff resistance and often severe persecution. When the Holy Spirit began to move in my own church, an irate member burned it down. Every truth that has been uncovered over the ages has been labeled by many detractors and traditionalists as a heresy, at best, and satanic, at worst. But God will have His way and the church moves on. There is always a remnant of people who are such seekers after God that they are willing to walk in obedience to the light God has given them, no matter what the price. And many have paid with their lives. I have often thought of Martin Luther and the persecution he endured when he moved out of tradition and ritual and spoke the truth that had been mostly lost for centuries, "The just shall live by faith." It certainly seemed radical at the time, but I am thankful for his obedience.

And I know that Davidic praise and worship may seem radical to some of you, for it certainly did to me. But if you will continue to press on with me, I believe that the Lord will open up the Word to you on this exciting subject.

Jesus told us to occupy until He returned. That word *occupy* in Greek is *pragmatĕuŏmai*, and it means "to busy oneself; to trade; to occupy," from a root word meaning "business." I have heard this term defined "to do business as usual." Shall we?

Heavenly Father, thank You that You are the King of Kings and the Lord of Lords. Thank You that You are sovereign and nothing happens apart from your permissive will. Father, we ask You to forgive us— your church—for our disobedience throughout the ages. As Nehemiah confessed and repented for the sins of the whole nation of Israel, we repent right now for the sins of the Body of Christ. Lord, we are not capable, in ourselves, of humble, unconditional love for one another. Please, Lord, convict us of the sins of pride, unbelief, self-righteousness, gossip, backbiting, strife, and divisiveness. Give us the grace to see with your eyes, hear with your ears, love with your heart, touch with your hands, and walk with your feet. Incline our hearts to love as You love. In Jesus' lovely name. Amen.

What Was Lost
Is Being Restored

It is truly a thrilling thing to look at Christ's church in historical perspective and see that it does not conflict with Scripture. The Israelites went from darkness to light to darkness to light to darkness, and history reveals that our pattern in the church has been the same. And yet the Scriptures say that Jesus Christ will return for His church (2 Pet. 3:14) and she will be a spotless, radiant bride, a pure virgin (2 Cor. 11:2). Though it seems to me that the Lord has His work cut out for Himself, I believe that as He restores the keys to the kingdom—as He turns on all the lights—His purposes will be accomplished. It is so important to be open to the Lord as these marvelous phenomena occur so as not to reject His truths and miss the blessings of restoration . . . not the blessing of life after death but the blessings of participating in what He is doing in the world in these last days. The Lord has not "saved" us just to get us to heaven. No! He has saved us for His glory and purposes. We are His hands and feet. We are the visible expression of Him, and we need all of the keys of the kingdom to reflect Him to a lost world.

It was to Peter that our Lord gave the keys to the kingdom, and it was Peter who said in his second sermon after Pentecost that Jesus would return upon the restitution of all things, which God spoke of through His holy prophets since the world began (Acts 3:20–21). The word *restitution* in Greek is *apŏkatastasis*, and it means "restoration to a former state." At the time these

76

words were spoken, Peter had the full set of keys to the kingdom which Jesus had given to him (which had been spoken of through the prophets), but those were lost to all but a few during the Dark Ages. So I believe that not only must all the keys that Peter was speaking of at that time be restored, but all the things common to the first-century church must be restored as well. History confirms this to me as more than a personal opinion, for I see it has been happening and is continuing to happen all over the world today in enthusiastic preparation for the soon-coming Bridegroom.

This book is particularly concerned with what I believe to be one of the most important of the "keys," which is Davidic praise and worship. The basis for my strong belief has already been stated in the chapter, "In Earth As It Is in Heaven," but I would like to state it one more time. I believe praise and worship are the primary and most likely only activities in Heaven. (Please remember that there is no such thing as "time" in eternity. Therefore, there is no such thing as boredom or weariness.) Praise and worship have always been and they always will be.

With regard to this most important key to the kingdom, God spoke through the prophet Amos and said that a sign of the New Covenant would be the worldwide outreach to the gentiles and at the same time there would be a restoration of the tabernacle of David.

AMOS 9:11–12: "In that day will I raise up the tabernacle of David that is fallen, and close up the breaches thereof; and I will raise up his ruins, and I will build it as in the days of old: That they may possess the remnant of Edom, and of all the heathen (gentiles), which are called by my name, saith the Lord who doeth this."

And James in his argument before the Council at Jerusalem regarding whether gentiles must first be converted to Judaism before they could be "considered" Christians, quoted this very prophecy as substantiation for the fact that gentiles were very much a part of God's divine plan from the foundations of the world.

ACTS 15:13–17: "And after they had held their peace, James answered, saying, Men and brethren, hearken unto me. Simeon hath declared how God at the first did visit the Gentiles, to take out of them a people for his name. And **to this agree the words of the prophets;** as it is written, After this I will return, and will build again the tabernacle of David, which is fallen down; and I will build again the ruins thereof, and I will set it up: That the residue of (unsaved) men might seek after the Lord, and all the Gentiles, upon whom my name is called, saith the Lord, who doeth all these things."

We know from Scripture that God no longer dwells in the tabernacles and temples made with hands (Acts 17:24), though for a brief moment in time His Presence did dwell in the Holy of Holies of the tabernacle of Moses (Exod. 25:22 and Num. 5:3) and later in the tabernacle of David and the temple of Solomon. Under the New Covenant, the believer in Jesus Christ is God's dwelling place (1 Cor. 6:19). It is clear from Scripture that the tabernacle of Moses is first a pattern and shadow of the tabernacle in heaven (Heb. 9:11), 23–24), and second the pattern of The Way for the believer to enter into divine union with God. (It is also a shadow of Jesus Christ, but we will not study that in this book.) And it is abundantly clear from Amos 9:11–12 and Acts 15:13–17 that the tabernacle of David is the pattern for worship and praise in the New Testament church.

Before we take a look at what God revealed through the tabernacle of David, let us look at David himself. David was clearly not only a type of Christ in the Old Testament as King, but he was also a type of New Testament believer. He is the only one mentioned in the entire Old Testament who is said to have had the Holy Spirit upon him from the day he was anointed by God to the day he died.

1 SAMUEL 16:13: "Then Samuel took the horn of oil, and anointed him (David) in the midst of his brethren: and the spirit of the Lord came upon David from that day forward. . . ."

And though David broke both the letter and the spirit of the Law through his sin with Bathsheba, God saw a heart totally repentant of that sin, and David was deemed righteous by the Lord all of his life.

1 KINGS 15:5: ". . . David did that which was right in the eyes of the Lord, and turned not aside from any thing that he commanded him all the days of his life, save only in the matter of Uriah the Hittite."
1 KINGS 14:8: ". . . my servant David, who kept my commandments, and who followed me with all his heart, to do that only which was right in mine eyes." (See also 1 Kings 11:33-34).

Before we move to David's tabernacle, I think it is appropriate to point out once again that God is not looking for people who never sin, for then we would be perfect and that cannot happen as long as we live in this fallen world. No! I believe God is looking for **the heart of integrity**. That is what David had, and God says David had a heart after God (Acts 13:22).

1 KINGS 9:4: "And if thou wilt walk before me, **as David thy father walked,** in integrity of heart, and in uprightness, to do according to all that I have commanded thee. . . ."

The heart of integrity fears the Lord and consequently hates sin. When the heart of integrity "slips," it is greatly grieved. It repents in the dust and ashes and receives the chastening of the Lord with praise and wisdom. The heart of integrity sincerely *wants* to obey God every moment of the day and genuinely lives for that purpose. I do hope this helps to clear up some misconceptions and confusion. It is certainly the central issue in the life of any believer, whether Old Testament or New.

Now let's have a look at David's tabernacle, that wonderful prophetic view of the New Testament church. The picture we have of it in scripture, of course, begins with "David, and the elders of Israel, and the captains over thousands" bringing the Ark of the Covenant to Mount Zion. As they moved from the house of Obed-edom to the City of David, they sacrificed bulls and rams in obedience to God's commands, and the Word of God says that they traveled with great rejoicing, multitudes singing, shouting, playing musical instruments, all in praise to

God. And in the midst of this tumultuous sound and sight of joy, there was David, dancing and playing before the Lord. After arriving in Zion, this exuberant, extravagant praise and worship continued night and day around the Ark of the Covenant, for the Ark was no longer separated from the people but was, rather, placed in their midst. Truly this is a type of the New Testament church. It is truly a thrilling picture of the tabernacle of David and I suggest that you read it through thoroughly for yourself. (See 1 Chron. 15:25—16:43 and 2 Sam. 6:1–23.) Don't skim over it, but rather savor every word and phrase. Look up words in the Hebrew to get a greater vision of what took place. As we were caught up in John's Revelation and the heavenly praise and worship, allow yourself to participate in the joyful noise of David and his kingdom in praise and worship to God. It's very apparent, isn't it, that there is little distinguishable difference between them? And this, David's tabernacle, is that to which Amos the prophet and James were referring. Throughout the centuries, men have praised God in this way. The Old Testament believers praised this way, and so did the Apostles and the early church built by them. We are told that the hosts of heaven praise God in this way. It was only after the church fell into darkness in the Middle Ages that the joyful sound stopped, and I believe it is God's great desire and requirement that it be restored before Jesus returns. And it is interesting that He has already begun to restore it all over the world today. That is strong evidence to me of the validity of this truth and that the return of our Lord may be soon. Very soon, though the finished work has yet to be revealed.

All I know is that I don't want to miss out on that joy. I want to be a part of the restoration in the church and from the church to the world.

O Lord, I want to understand the Truth of this. Give me your wisdom and understanding. Bring it to light for me. Lord, I hunger and thirst after You. I seek You with all my heart, that I may know You and praise and worship You in spirit and in truth. Teach me, Lord. Cause your rivers of living waters to flow forth from my heart. Let me taste of your sweet Shekinah Glory, Lord. Give me a greater and greater revelation of Yourself, Sweet Lord! For it is in Jesus' name that I pray. Amen.

Finding Lost Treasure

The King James Version of the Bible is wonderful and I love it, but any halfway serious student of the Bible knows that buried away beneath the English translations in any of the versions, there is an abundance of hidden treasure, particularly in the Old Testament texts that are written in Hebrew. The Hebrew language is uniquely expressive, often painting an entire picture with one word. This is particularly true when it comes to the subject we are studying. There are seven root words in Hebrew which are all translated "praise" but have dramatically different meanings. Studying these words and seeing them used in a verse will give us a clearer picture of what is lost in translation as opposed to what God intended. (Some of these we have already looked at, but I have included them here for easier comparison.)

- *hâlal:* to be clear (of sound); to shine; hence to make a show, to boast; and thus to be (clamorously) foolish; to rave; to celebrate; to stultify. (Ps. 113:1, 3, "Praise *[hâlal]* ye the Lord. Praise *[hâlal]*, O ye servants of the Lord, praise *[hâlal]* the name of the Lord. From the rising of the sun unto the going down of the same, the Lord's name is to be praised *[hâlal*(ed)].")
- *t'hillâh:* to sing *hâlals;* to sing praises extravagantly; to celebrate with song. From the root word *hâlal.* (Ps. 147:1, "Praise *[hâlal]* ye the Lord: for it is good to sing

praises *[t'hillâh]* unto our God; for it is pleasant; and praise *[t'hillâh]* is comely.")

* *zamar:* to touch the strings (of an instrument); to celebrate with song and music. (Ps. 57:7, "My heart is fixed, O God, my heart is fixed: I will sing and give praise *[zâmar]*.")

* *yâdâh:* to revere or worship (with extended hands). (Ps. 67:3, "Let the people praise *[yâdâh]* thee, O God; let all the people praise *[yâdâh]* thee.")

* *tôwdâh:* to extend the hands (usually in adoration); confession; (sacrifice of) praise, thanks (giving, offering). (Ps. 50:23, "Whoso offereth praise *[tôdâh]* glorifieth me. . . .")

* *shâbach:* to address in a loud tone; glory; praise; triumph (to shout [in triumph] praises to God—my understanding.) (Ps. 145:4, "One generation shall praise *[shâbach]* thy works to another, and shall declare thy mighty acts.")

* *bârak:* to kneel; by implication to bless God (as an act of adoration). (Ps. 72:15, "And he shall live, and to him shall be given of the gold of Sheba: prayer also shall be made for him continually; and daily shall he be praised *[bârak*(ed)]*.")

We can certainly look at the definitions of these root words and see that praise is far more demonstrative than we thought. In addition to these hidden nuggets that are lost in translation, there are many clear commands to participate in the numerous aspects of praise which are patently and openly demonstrative in nature. I would be remiss in not pointing out a few of them.

PSALM 98:4,6: "Make a joyful noise unto the Lord, all the earth; make a loud noise, and rejoice, and sing praise. . . . With trumpets and sound of cornet make a joyful noise before the Lord, the King."

PSALM 32:11: "Be glad in the Lord, and rejoice, ye righteous; and shout for joy, all ye that are upright in heart."

PSALM 96:1–2: "Oh, sing unto the Lord a new song; sing unto the Lord, all the earth. Sing unto the Lord, bless his name; show forth his salvation from day to day."

PSALM 47:1: "O clap your hands, all ye peoples; shout unto God with the voice of triumph."
PSALM 63:4: "Thus will I bless thee while I live: I will lift up my hands in thy name."

The lifting of the hands is a particularly important compo-nent of praise for me, for it takes humility and surrender of the flesh to get those hands up there for everyone to see. At first they feel like television antennas. But the lifting of the hands is not some meaningless physical exercise in the presence of God. It expresses worship from the heart. And let me ask this question. When a little child wants attention from a parent, what is the first thing he does? He walks up to mother or daddy and lifts his hands to be picked up. This analogy can be applied to our heavenly Father as well.

One day as I was meditating on the lifting up of the hands to the Lord, I saw myself standing in praise to God with my hands extended heavenward, and I saw the Shekinah glory of God descend between those uplifted arms, much as is described in the Bible when the glory of God's Presence came to rest between the wings of the cherubim on the mercy seat in the tabernacle. It was as if God were saying, "You are, as a believer, indwelled by my Holy Spirit. I am the propitiation for your sins. I am your mercy seat, and I am in you. Your uplifted arms are your body's counterpart to the outstretched wings of the cherubim. As you praise me, I will enthrone myself and my glory upon you."

There is much that has been lost in the translation from the Hebrew and Greek, and the seven root words for praise mentioned earlier are a clear example of that. It is so important that we dig deep into the Word of God for the hidden treasure that is there, for the full intent of God's heart and desire.

For the first few years of my early Christian growth I read those thousands of references to praise and worship and failed to grasp their true meaning, and this same thing may be true in the lives of many believers. This is a great loss to our Lord and to us as well. Davidic praise and worship are a mutually great and awesome blessing. Apart from the blessing the believer receives, I believe the Scriptures show that we who are not taking part in this ministry to God are not responding to the many, many commands and calls in the Bible to worship and praise as David did.

I would like to share just a few more insights into the word of God on this subject that I have found helpful. To begin with, let's look at Psalm 22:3. "But thou art holy, O thou that inhabitest the praises of Israel." The Hebrew word for "inhabitest" is *yâshab*, and it translates, "to sit down (specifically as judge, in quiet); by implication to dwell, to remain; to settle, to marry; to abide; to dwell." The *New American Standard Bible* translates this verse, ". . . O Thou who art enthroned upon the praises of Israel." The same Hebrew word *yâshab* is used in Psalm 80:1. "Give ear, O Shepherd of Israel, thou that leadest Joseph like a flock; thou that dwellest between the cherubim, shine forth." The NASB translates that ". . . Thou who art **enthroned** above the cherubim. . . ." We can also find this same use of the word *yâshab* and its alternate translation in the NASB in Psalm 99:1 and Isaiah 37:16. Considering the mercy seat, which is covered by the cherubim in the Holy of Holies, to be a type of God's throne, I prefer the translation, "enthroned upon." From these verses, I conclude that praise is God's dwelling place, His throne. As we meditate upon the scriptures in Revelation, we can clearly see that there is continual praise and worship around the throne of God, but this scripture says more than that. It says to me that praise and worship **are** God's throne. Let's think about this. As we lift our hearts, our hands and our voices in praise to God, He enthrones Himself in our midst. God's presence evokes worship. It is really so clear to me. If I had not come to understand how the church fell into darkness and lost the keys to the kingdom, I would be most confused about how we could have lost sight of this marvelous truth, for it is something God's people have always known.

Another example of the same spiritual principle is the Hebrew word *nâvâh*, which translates "to rest (as at home); to celebrate (with praises); prepare an habitation." This word contains so much wisdom. To me it says once again, just as Psalm 22:3 does, that God's resting place is praise. Let's look at a verse where this word *nâvâh* appears: "Thou in thy mercy hast led forth the people which thou hast redeemed: thou hast guided them in thy strength unto thy holy habitation" (Exod.

15:13). There is a great wealth of buried treasure in this verse, beginning with the word *habitation*, for this is *nâvâh*, not only in God's holy habitation but a celebration of praises to Him. I pray that I am adequately expressing this so that you might receive the full revelation of it. However, where I am inadequate, I believe the Holy Spirit is able to reveal the precious truth of this to you. We see once again that praise is God's dwelling place.

In search of more buried treasure, hidden nuggets of God's truth, let's look at the word *strength*, which also appears in Exodus 15:13. That word in Hebrew is *'ôwz*, and it means "strength in various applications (force, security, majesty, praise): boldness, loud, might, power, strength, strong." This is the same Hebrew word that appears in Psalm 8:2: "Out of the mouth of babes and sucklings hast thou ordained strength because of thine enemies, that thou mightest still the enemy and the avenger." This is the same verse Jesus quoted in Matthew 21:16, but instead of translating the word "strength" as David did, Jesus put the emphasis on praise: ". . . Yea; have ye never read, Out of the mouth of babes and sucklings thou hast perfected **praise**?" The surprising correlation here is that God's strength within us and our praise of Him are one and the same. They are as closely interrelated as God's dwelling place and praise. I have so prayed that the Holy Spirit would enable me to put this into words that would set your heart on fire, a fire that will never go out again.

I strongly believe that this word *'owz* has a counterpart in the New Testament, and that is the Greek word *dunamis*, which translates "force; specifically miraculous power (usually by implication a miracle itself)." The reason I believe these two words hold the same implication is the verse in Revelation 4:11 in which John seems to use the word *power* where *praise* would seem more appropriate: "Thou art worthy, O Lord, to receive glory and honour and **power**." I believe praise and God's miracle-working power are so closely related that they are almost one and the same. In fact, I not only believe it but have seen the truth of it. I also believe that this is the key of the kingdom that will restore the other lost keys to the Body of Christ in the last days before the return of Christ. That is why I feel the Lord has called me to write this book—to stir up the hearts of His people that He might open their eyes and set their hearts ablaze with praise and worship.

I think it is appropriate here to tell you of one of the many personal, eyewitness experiences I have had with this mighty, miracle-working *dunamis* power of God that falls in the midst of Davidic praise and worship. One Sunday after I first began to attend Shady Grove Church, I took my daughter, Wendy, and her husband, Brad, with me. I could not help noticing that Brad was not only **not** participating (he was standing in a rather frozen condition), but that he was extremely uncomfortable. Having felt the same way myself during my first few exposures to extravagant praise and worship, I prayed for him and continued to praise the Lord. In a few moments, the congregation became quite still and a "word of knowledge" (1 Cor. 12:8) came through a member of the body. This is the word of the Lord to the best of my recollection: "There is someone here today who feels he can never love the Lord the way he sees us loving Him. This person is bewildered about this great demonstration of love pouring forth to the Lord. Won't you please come forward and let us pray for you?" Well, I knew this word was for my son-in-law. My spirit bore witness to that, but it was not up to me to tell him, so I prayed for him.

Brad did not respond. A few moments later, the same word came forth again. No response. Yet a third time the word was uttered to no avail. My son-in-law stood frozen. Now I cannot say that I did not understand his reluctance to respond, because I have felt that resistance of pride in me when there has been a call for me to go forward. My pride did not want me to be exposed as less than what I appeared to be before other believers. (After much struggle, I believe the Lord has broken me of that. How foolish to resist ministry for my burdens and problems! That's what body ministry is all about!) However, in Brad's case it was not that he was too proud to respond; the problem was far deeper than that. He did not even know that the call to come forward for prayer was for him. So we left the church that morning without the Lord touching his hurt and confusion, and I continued to pray intensely for him.

On Wednesday night at our home Bible study, he and Wendy could not wait to tell me what had happened. On

Monday evening, my son-in-law had been taking a shower when the voice of the Lord rang deep in his heart. It said, "Brad, that was you I was speaking to in church Sunday. That was you I was calling to come forward. You are the one whose heart is so hard that you feel you can never love me as you saw the people in that church loving me. Brad, go forth in church next Sunday. Humble yourself before me and before your brothers and sisters in Christ. I will heal you of this hardness and I will heal you of your hurt." Brad went to church the following Sunday, but he still held back. It took one more word from the Lord to get him out of his frozen stance with the Lord. A woman got up to say, "There is someone here today who thinks he can never love the Lord the way he sees us loving Him. He is blaming God for something that is not God's fault. Please come forward that you might be healed." At this point, Brad jumped out of his place and ran to the front of the church. He received prayer and today he is healed. Today he and Wendy worship in spirit and in truth in the same church where Clint and I worship, and they live to love and serve the Lord.

This is just one of many examples of what happens in the midst of praise and worship for the common good of the whole body. There is salvation. There is healing and deliverance for the believer. Marriages are healed and strengthened. People leave church with great hope and a sense of relief, knowing that God has met their needs that day. In so many churches today, people come to the services hurting and burdened with problems, and they leave feeling the same way. I believe God meets His people in praise and worship and those who come hurting leave knowing they have been touched and that their burdens have been eased. They leave with hope.

Before we leave this word 'ôwz, I would like to call your attention to one more thing. The Ark of the Testimony in the Holy of Holies is also referred to as the Ark of the Covenant, the Ark of God, the Ark of the Lord, and the Ark of thy **Strength.** The word for "strength" here is 'ôwz. Thus the Ark of the Covenant is the Ark of Strength/Praise. Psalm 132:7–9 beautifully embodies all that I have been saying about praise and worship, God's habitation and strength: "We will go into his tabernacles: we will worship at his footstool. Arise, O Lord, into thy **rest;** thou, and the ark of thy strength. Let thy priests be clothed with righteousness; and let thy saints shout for joy." God's resting place is praise and worship. The Ark of God is strength and praise. And Psalm 8:2 also incorporates praise with the victorious power of God over all the power of the enemy: "Out of the mouths of babes and sucklings hast thou ordained strength (praise) because of thine enemies, **that thou mightest still the enemy and the avenger.**" These are certainly and most definitely eternal truths of God, my friend. O that we might be caught up into the heart of God on this matter! O that we might have the eye salve of the Holy Spirit to see this truth as God intends.

One last nugget from Exodus 15:13. It reads, "Thou in thy mercy hast led forth the people which thou hast redeemed: thou hast guided them in thy strength unto thy holy habitation." The word *guided* in Hebrew is *nâhal,* meaning "to run with a sparkle, i.e., flow; hence to conduct; to protect, sustain: carry, feed, guide, lead (gently, on)." Here once again we see an aspect of God's character that is most different from my personal concept of God. We see Him "running with sparkle" ahead of His people, leading them gently on in His "strength/ praise" to His holy "habitation/celebration of praise." This one verse gives us deep spiritual insight into the desires of God's heart and character. It makes my heart rejoice. You too can study these words in *Strong's Exhaustive Concordance of the Bible* and receive enrichment in the wisdom of God. Then you may find yourself singing, as David did, "More to be desired are they than gold, yea, than much fine gold; sweeter also than honey and the honeycomb."

In light of what God's word says about these things, we can see we have definitely fallen short of the glory of God. Our rational temperament, derived to a great extent from Northern European culture, tends to be undemonstrative and controlled, which is what our sociological background interprets as dignified, poised and sophisticated.

By contrast, it is very interesting to observe the open and demonstrative nature of the Jewish people. They worship God in this way. They love their families and friends this way. They are expressive and bold, and this seems to be how God created them to be toward Himself. If you attend a Jewish wedding you will see this gaiety and joy in Jewish people even today, but in our poised, dignified culture, it is not often acceptable to show our emotions. Except, of course, at football games, boxing matches, bullfights, rock concerts, sad movies, etc. Isn't it interesting that our emotions must be vented somewhere, and the only place we have permission (of society and cultural background) to do that is at events which are violent to one degree or another, or maudlin? Our emotions come out in very unacceptable forms of violence as well—murder, rape, sadomasochism, temper tantrums, gossip, etc. Are we going to continue to let Satan get away with this, possibly the greatest robbery of all mankind? Satan has robbed God and His church of the whole purpose of creation—to praise and worship the Lord. He has not only gotten away with robbery for far too long, but he has succeeded in perverting what was pure and lovely and subverting it for his own destructive purposes.

Let's ask the Lord to forgive us and lead us in the way we should go. He is extending one of the lost keys to the kingdom to us. Let's reach out boldly and take it.

Heavenly Father, we come before your throne, humbly but boldly, for mercy and grace to help in this time of need. We confess to You that we have not praised You according to your Word. We ask that You teach us, that we might become worshipers in spirit and in truth, for we confess we don't even know where to begin. We lift our hands to You. We open our mouths and sing a love song to You. We clap an offering of praise to your name. Help us, O Lord. Set our spirits free to worship You and be a sweet, joyful sound in your ear. You have not given us a spirit of fear, but of love, power, and a sound mind. It is in your name, Jesus, that we pray. Amen.

But That's Old Testament!

After I was born again and had been a Christian for awhile, the Lord led me to a Bible study where the people praised the Lord the way we are told David did. I confess to you that at first I felt quite awkward. I didn't know the songs, and the clapping and lifting of the hands were something I had never been exposed to, but it didn't take me long to begin to enjoy it and look forward to it very much. At the same time I was exposed to lots of Christian groups and organizations, and I saw that not everyone praised the Lord in this manner. I began to question why and discovered that a lot of people didn't believe in it, for many reasons. Some believed that it was strictly an Old Testament thing. Others just didn't feel comfortable with the open display of love and adoration toward the Lord, and, as I said earlier, I think that is partly our cultural and social background in America. Still others were repulsed by what they considered to be overemotionalism.

The question that kept arising in my mind was, "What happened?" I knew Davidic praise and worship were meaningful in my Christian growth. If the Scriptures teach that praise is active, expressive, demonstrative, clamorous, and that worship is expressed in body posture that reflects the heart, then why is it such an alien thing to so many of us?

Certainly the Old Testament has much more to say on the subject than the New. But there is a lot more in the New Testament than I was ever aware of until I began to study it, and the New Testament was largely written by Jews who were part of the Old Testament dispensation. When Paul wrote to Timothy that "all scripture is given by inspiration of God, and is profitable for doctrine, for reproof, for correction, for instruction in righteousness: That the man of God may be perfect, thoroughly furnished unto all good works" (2 Tim. 3:16–17), he was referring to the Old Testament, for those were the only Scriptures they had at that time. In fact, in verse 15 Paul clearly alludes to these Scriptures that we know today as the "Old" Testament. The New Testament is the Old revealed. The Old Testament is the New concealed. God has not changed His game plan. He is merely moving progressively to bring it to pass. The Bible says He is the same yesterday, today and forever, and that He does not change. We need both Testaments of the Bible for our spiritual maturity.

The writers of the New Testament relied heavily on the scriptures of the Old Testament. Matthew, Mark, Luke, John, the inspired author of the letter to the Hebrews, James, Peter, and Jude all were avid students of the Old Testament and quoted it liberally in their writings. Jesus quoted it and taught from it every day of His ministry.

How can the Old Testament be a book that is closed or of little importance to Christians when much of the prophecy contained therein remains unfulfilled until the return of Jesus Christ? There are approximately 1800 Bible passages concerned with the second coming of Jesus Christ. It is not and cannot be a closed book! It is serious error to omit it from our studies and to discount the validity and importance of what it has to say for our lives today. Jesus said, "Think not that I am come to destroy the law, or the prophets: I am not come to destroy, but to fulfil. For verily I say unto you, Till heaven and earth pass, one jot or one tittle shall in no wise pass from the law, till all be fulfilled" (Matt. 5:17–18).

Christ was the end of the law for righteousness to everyone that believes in Him (Rom. 10:4), but the truths of the Old Testament consist of spiritual laws and principles that apply to us today. There is a profundity of revelation of God's character and attributes contained therein that if overlooked or discounted would be a great loss to us. It is pure beauty in its content and glorious in its promise. Listen to what it has to say. Ask the Holy Spirit to teach you. He will!

I know that many of you reading this book understand what I am saying and may even be wondering why I am belaboring the point, but I have met many, many people who do **not** understand and have, therefore, never touched the Old Testament. For this reason I would like to spend a little time establishing the point. Besides, there are many interesting things you may never have seen before that would be helpful to you if you encounter this situation. I am always eager to learn and build upon what I already know; aren't you?

Jesus taught constantly from the Old Testament. The Gospels are full of those teachings. After His resurrection, as He walked along with two of His disciples on the road to Emmaus, He taught them from the Scriptures.

Luke 24:26–27" "Ought not Christ to have suffered these things, and to enter into his glory? And beginning at Moses and all the prophets, he expounded unto them in **all** the scriptures the things **concerning himself.**"

And, though the disciples at the time did not know it was the Messiah, they responded to what He had to say to them, much as I respond today as I search the Scriptures and the Holy Spirit gives wisdom and revelation.

Luke 24:32: ". . . Did not our heart burn within us, while he talked with us by the way, and while he opened to us the scriptures?"

These disciples later had their eyes opened and saw that their teacher was the risen Lord Himself, and He said to them once again . . .

Luke 24:44–45: ". . . These are the words which I spake unto you, while I was yet with you, that all things must be fulfilled, which were written in the law of Moses, and in the prophets, and in the psalms, **concerning me.** Then opened he their understanding, that they might understand the scriptures."

Paul stressed that the Old Testament Scriptures were for our edification and learning.

ROMANS 15:4: "For whatsoever things were written aforetime were written **for our learning**. . . ."

1 CORINTHIANS 10:11–12: "Now all these things happened (in the Old Testament) unto them for ensamples: and they are written **for our admonition,** upon whom the ends of the world are come. Wherefore let him that thinketh he standeth take heed lest he fall."

ACTS 24:14: ". . . this I confess unto thee, that after the way (Jesus) which they call heresy, so worship I the God of my fathers, **believing all things** which are written in the law and in the prophets."

The Psalmist wrote in the Old Testament: "This shall be written **for the generation to come:** and the people which shall be **created** shall praise *(hâlal)* the Lord" (102:18). Who was the Psalmist referring to? Who are the people who **shall be created?** I am convinced that this verse must pertain to the new creature in Christ referred to in 2 Corinthians 5:17, for until such time as Jesus Christ entered into the world to save sinners, there was only **one** creation. (If you are not a regular student of the Old Testament, you are missing so much.)

Regarding the eternal spiritual truth of praise, the Psalmist wrote that the people who shall be created (the new creatures) **shall** praise the Lord. But even more clearly for you New Testament lovers, Paul wrote that the gentiles would praise the Lord, quoting Old Testament scripture as his authority.

ROMANS 15:4–11: "For whatsoever things were written aforetime were written for our learning, that we through patience and comfort of the scriptures might have hope. Now the God of patience and consolation grant you to be like-minded one toward another (Jew and gentile) according to Christ Jesus: That ye may with one mind and one mouth **glorify God,** even the Father of our Lord Jesus Christ. Wherefore receive ye one another, as Christ also received us to the glory of God. Now I say that Jesus Christ was a minister of the circumcision (Jews) for the truth of God, **to confirm the promises made unto the fathers** (in the Old Testament): And **that the gentiles might glorify God** for his mercy; as it is written (in the Old Testament, Ps. 18:49), For this cause I will confess to thee among the Gentiles, and **sing unto thy name.** And again he (the prophet Moses, Deut. 32:43) saith, Rejoice, ye Gentiles, with his people. And again (in the Old Testament, Ps. 117:1), Praise the Lord, all ye Gentiles; and laud him all ye peoples."

Let's examine more closely what those Old Testament references that Paul quoted say in the Hebrew regarding praise.

PSALM 18:49: "Therefore will I give thanks *(yâdâh)* unto thee, O Lord, among the heathen, and sing praises *(hâlal)* unto thy name." (Cf. Rom. 15:9.)

DEUTERONOMY 32:43: "Rejoice (shout), O ye nations (gentiles): **with his people** (the Jews): for he will avenge the blood of his servants, and will render vengeance to his adversaries, and will be merciful unto his land, and to his people." (Cf. Rom. 15:10.)

PSALM 117:1: "Oh, praise *(hâlal)* the Lord, all ye nations (gentiles): praise *(shâbach)* him, all ye people." (Cf. Rom. 15:11.)

Luke also quoted David's prophecy regarding the death and resurrection of the Messiah and the praise that sprang forth from his heart in exultation in response to such a promise.

ACTS 2:25–28: "For David speaketh concerning him (the Messiah), I foresaw the Lord always before my face, for he is on my right hand, that I should not be moved: Therefore did my heart rejoice, and my tongue was glad; moreover also my flesh shall rest in hope: Because thou will not leave my soul in hell, neither wilt thou suffer thine Holy One to see corruption. Thou hast made known to me the ways of life; thou shalt make me **full of joy** with thy countenance."

Let's see what the Psalm that Luke quoted reveals.

PSALM 16:8–10: "I have set the Lord always before me: because he is at my right hand, I shall not be moved. Therefore my heart is glad, and my glory rejoiceth *(gûwl:* to spin round [under the influence of any violent emotion], i.e., usually rejoice): my flesh also shall rest in hope. For thou wilt not leave my soul in hell; neither wilt thou suffer thine Holy One to see corruption."

Should we, who live with the reality of that resurrection of Jesus Christ within us, respond any less than David did when the promised Good News was revealed to him? I pray that God will have mercy upon us, His church, and begin to open our eyes to the truth.

HEBREWS 13:15–16: "By him therefore let us offer the sacrifice of praise to God **continually,** that is, the fruit of our lips giving thanks to his name. But to do good and to communicate forget not: for with such sacrifices God is well pleased."

EPHESIANS 5:17–21: "Wherefore be ye not unwise, but understanding what **the will of the Lord is.** And be not drunk with wine, wherein is excess; but be filled with the Spirit; **speaking to yourselves in psalms and hymns and spiritual songs, singing and making melody in your heart to the Lord;** Giving thanks always for all things unto God and the Father in the name of our Lord Jesus Christ; Submitting yourselves one to another in the fear of God."

PHILIPPIANS 3:3: ". . . We are the circumcision, **which worship God in the spirit, and rejoice in Christ Jesus,** and have no confidence in the flesh."

COLOSSIANS 3:16: "Let the word of Christ dwell in you richly in all wisdom; teaching and admonishing one another in psalms and hymns and spiritual songs, singing with grace in your hearts to the Lord."

Psalms! That must mean that they are for our instruction and example. The Book of Psalms was the Hebrew hymnal, and we are spiritual Jews. They are for our examples. They are good "for doctrine, reproof, correction and instruction in righteousness."

PSALM 150: "Praise (the Hebrew word for *praise* throughout this psalm is *hâlal)* ye the Lord. Praise God in his sanctuary: praise him in the firmament of his power. Praise him for his mighty acts: praise him according to his excellent greatness. Praise him with the sound of the trumpet: praise him with the psaltery and harp. Praise him with the timbrel and dance: praise him with stringed instruments and flutes. Praise him upon the loud cymbals; praise him upon the high sounding cymbals. Let everything that hath breath praise the Lord. Praise ye the Lord."

Father God, we pray that You will illuminate the Scriptures for us as we meditate in them. We ask that You cause our hearts to burn within us and cause us to understand. Reveal all that You have for us each day and enlarge our capacity for wisdom and understanding. Enlarge our capacity for You and for knowing You. Point the way that we should walk. In Jesus' name. Amen.

The Lion of Judah

REVELATION 5:5: "... behold, the Lion of the tribe of Judah ..."

What significance those words hold for the believer in Jesus Christ! Jesus is the Lion of Judah, and He defeated Satan when He rose from the dead (1 John 3:8, Col. 2:15 and John 12:31). This victory over Satan and death is the very essence of the Gospel of Jesus Christ, and every believer's heart is filled with gratitude in the knowledge of what Jesus did on the cross. But there are several powerful spiritual principles in this name for Jesus—the Lion of the tribe of Judah—that are relevant to the vast and wonderful subject of Davidic praise and worship. I would like to look at three of those spiritual principles: (1) Praise overcomes the enemy. (2) Praise overcomes our flesh (carnal, ungodly desires). (3) Therefore, praise and worship bring us into right relationship with the Lord, and the rivers of living water begin to flow forth from us in abundance.

First I would like to examine the symbolism of the name "the Lion of the tribe of Judah." The most obvious, of course, is the lion's image as the king of the jungle. He is strong, fierce, noble, stately, and his roar is tremendous. He is also carnivorous. The second, and more subtle, lies hidden away in the Hebrew definition of this name of Jesus, "Judah." Judah in Hebrew is Y'hûwdâh, which means "celebrated; praise to God." The root word, yâdâh, as you may recall, means "to revere or

97

worship with extended hands." But there is even more significance in the phrase "tribe of Judah," for Judah was the tribe
which camped in front of the gate (The Way) of the tabernacle.
How beautifully this illustration fits with the words of the
psalmist, "Enter into his gates with thanksgiving (*yâdâh*), and
into his courts with praise (*t*²*hillâh*)" (Ps. 100:4). It is also very
important to note that as Israel went into battle, it was always
the tribe of Judah that led the way. God never wastes anything
in His Word. Everything is important. These are strong
principles of great significance to our Christian lives, not even
subtly hidden. God places an extremely high priority on
Davidic praise and worship. I believe the Scriptures reveal
these are His highest priority once we have been saved. (After
all, the dead cannot praise the Lord.)

Let's examine the first spiritual principle—praise overcomes
the enemy. We have already seen in the study of Psalm 8:2 that
strength/praise is ordained of God that we might overcome the
enemy and the avenger. There is no greater demonstration of
this truth in the Bible than the much-quoted passage in 2
Chronicles 20:1–30. Here we find all of Judah discovering the
news that a great multitude of people from Ammon, Moab, and
Mount Seir were coming against them and their King,
Jehoshaphat, in battle. They were greatly afraid and "set
themselves to seek the Lord." They first gathered together,
fasted, and began to pray and seek the help of the Lord. They
began to praise and speak of God and of His wonderful and
awesome deeds. They recognized that God was their only help.
In the midst of this powerful prayer meeting, the Spirit of the
Lord spoke, saying, "Be not afraid nor dismayed by reason of
this great multitude; for the battle is not yours, but God's. . . .
Ye shall not need to fight in this battle; set yourselves, stand ye
still, and see the salvation of the Lord with you, O Judah and
Jerusalem. Fear not, nor be dismayed. Tomorrow go out against
them; for the Lord will be with you. And Jehoshaphat **bowed
his head and face to the ground:** and **all** Judah and the
inhabitants of Jerusalem **fell before the Lord, worshiping the
Lord.** . . . [they] **stood up to praise** (*hâlal*) **the Lord God of
Israel with a loud voice on high.**" Then they arose the next
morning and went forth. Jehoshaphat reminded his people to

"believe in the Lord, your God. So shall you be established. Believe his prophets, so shall you prosper." He then appointed singers to praise the beauty of God's holiness. The praisers went before the army. As they began to sing and praise the Lord, the Lord set an ambush against Ammon, Moab, and Mount Seir, and they destroyed one another. Without their having lifted anything but their voices, the multitude of their enemy was smitten. In fact, it was in the lifting of their voices in praise to God that the strength of God was manifested and the enemy and the avenger were overcome, in perfect accordance with Psalm 8:2.

To me, the key to victory over the enemy through praise is in the God we praise. As the people of Judah went out to battle, Jehoshaphat called upon them to "believe in the Lord your God . . . believe his prophets." Believe all they have to say about the Lord!

These people did believe and they knew their God. They went forth in the natural outflow of that knowledge of Him, which is praise to Him. We can only praise and worship God to the degree that we know Him. In *Worship—The Missing Jewel of the Evangelical Church*, A. W. Tozer says, "You cannot worship a Being you cannot trust. Confidence is necessary to respect, and respect is necessary to worship. Worship rises or falls in any church altogether depending upon the attitude we take toward God, whether we see God big or whether we see Him little." We cannot trust a God we do not know. And we cannot praise a God we do not know. Praise for the sake of praise is just another clanging cymbal, just another fleshly act.

Rare—very rare—is the day in my life when I do not make time to praise and worship the Lord. This is a great source of joy and comfort to me, not a burdensome duty. And I see a real difference in my growth and maturity as a result of this commitment. God gets bigger and bigger to me every day. And He demonstrates His power through my life in numerous and various ways every day.

Two fresh examples come to my mind. I was recently traveling with a new Christian friend, and she was sharing many of her burdens with me. Until recently she had had a relationship with Jesus that was at her convenience. (Those were her words, not mine.) I say that so that you will understand what I am about to say. As we talked she began to share with me that her husband was dying of cancer. To make matters worse, he was suffering from acute heart failure and was not expected to live much longer. She was trembling and weeping as we talked. We were traveling with a large group of Christians on an important semi-diplomatic mission that potentially could open up the entire Arab world to the Gospel of Christ. So even though her husband had been quite ill for some time, they both felt it was essential that she be on this trip. They felt it was worth the risk.

It is always interesting to see how God reveals to those who are listening ways in which He wants to demonstrate His great power and love. Suddenly this lady began telling me things she probably had not intended to say. As our conversation flowed on, she confided that two years before she had been called by a fortune teller who said he wanted to see her. (This woman is prominent and well known. The fortune teller was visiting her city and had gotten her name from one of her friends. Isn't it interesting that Satan came like a roaring lion, seeking to devour. She did not go to him; he came to her!)

This clairvoyant's *modus operandi* was to look at photographs of those people important in your life and then tell the future of each one. As my friend laid out her pictures, he began to do this. At the conclusion of his session with her, she realized that he had not mentioned her husband. Finally she pinned him down and said, "You still have not mentioned my husband." The man's response was, "Forget him. He'll be dead in two years. He will contract cancer, but he will die of heart failure before the cancer kills him." Two months later, her husband, who had been perfectly healthy, was diagnosed with terminal cancer.

I can only tell you that I was immediately quickened in my spirit by God to say, "This is a curse from the devil. It can be broken in Jesus' name." I then showed her in Galatians 3:13 and Colossians 2:14–15 that Jesus had "become a curse for us" and had taken every curse against us to the cross with Him. She renounced this sin and sought God's forgiveness and cleansing. We then claimed those promises from the Word of God in Jesus' name.

She told me that it had been difficult to accept that she would have to give her husband up but that she knew there was no hope. She felt sure that he was going to die. I assured her that God does heal and that I believed God for that. This time of prayer with her did not seem to me to be a great and powerful one. The prayer was simple. I didn't even pray for healing. It just didn't occur to me (I believe, so that God, would receive all the glory). I merely confessed to her that I believed that God heals. I tell you this so you will know that what happened did not happen because of the quality of my prayer with her. It was not me; it was God.

When we arrived at our hotel, we went to our rooms, agreeing to join the group of people we were traveling with for a time of devotion before dinner. After a brief rest we all came together. We had been sharing and talking about the Lord for several minutes when the telephone rang. It was for my friend. She was out of the room about five minutes. When she returned, she came and sat down beside me and was very still for about two minutes. She could not contain herself any longer than that. In the middle of the devotional she reached over and grabbed my hand and whispered in my ear, "I have just got to tell you this! When I went to my room after talking to you, I was suddenly flooded from head to toe with an overwhelming sense of joy and peace. It was indescribable. And I heard this still small voice saying within me, 'Your husband is healed.'" She then told me that the telephone call had been from her husband. When she heard him say, "I've got something wonderful to tell you," she interrupted, "Don't tell me, let me tell you. You are cured." He asked her, "How did you know?" She then related to him what had happened.

Not every one of my prayers is answered that quickly and exactly in that way. I don't have all the answers. God's ways are a mystery that we cannot fully understand while we live on this earth, as we are told in 1 Corinthians 13:12. However, the Bible also says that God will reveal many mysteries and secrets to us if we abide in Him (Jer. 33:3, 1 Cor. 2:9–10). And I do believe that God always answers our prayers (I just don't always know how and when), so it's important to persevere (Luke 18:1).

One word of caution before we leave this subject. How naïvely we traipse off to such dangerous things as fortune tellers, astrologers, tarot card readers and the like. God warns us in His Word that these things and the like are abominations to Him, because these occult activities deal in the realm of demonic powers and forces. And yet many, many of us innocently enter into them, not realizing the serious consequences. My friend had no idea what she was playing around with!

Another recent example of the mighty power of God flowing out of my life of Davidic praise and worship is quite different but just as powerful in my eyes. When I began to pray for the salvation of my husband, I found myself including many of his friends, as well as mine. I saw in their lives all of the problems that I was having, and I knew that Jesus was the only answer to those problems. (We have seen many friends, business partners and employees come to the Lord in the past five years! What a thrill!) This recent answer to prayer involves one of my husband's old buddies. This friend has had a lot of heartaches in his life. I discern in him a deep sense of inadequacy and a very wounded spirit. I know personally that he has experienced a lot of rejection in his life. He was very much like I was before I met the Lord.

A few months ago when the Dallas Cowboys were in Los Angeles to play the Rams on a Monday night, we had the opportunity of being with this friend for two consecutive evenings. The second evening, we were riding a bus to the ball game with a large group of friends and acquaintances. Because of traffic, that bus trip took us four hours. We arrived when the game was almost half over. But I see the providential hand of God (I call it "the fingerprints of God") all over that time.

This friend was with a young woman that he was "madly" in love with, but she was living with someone else. He was mooning and pining away for her. What consciously caused him to get up and come sit next to me (Clint was mixing among his friends on the bus), I will never know. I say consciously, because I know that the Lord drew him to the seat next to me. We have never talked. We have never been particularly friendly, so it had to be the Lord!

He began to tell me all of his problems . . . how he just knew this young woman with him was **the** right one for him (how often he must have said that over the years!). He was drinking and was quite melancholy. I began to share my testimony with him. I told him that I believed no one could ever find contentment, peace, and joy in life apart from a relationship with Jesus Christ. As we talked, I asked him if he would pray with me for Jesus to come into his life. Within thirty minutes, this man had opened his heart to Jesus.

We continued to talk about the Lord for the remainder of those four hours, in a crowded bus on a traffic-jammed freeway. I offered to find a Bible study for him and he said, "No!" He also told me not to tell anyone that he had asked Jesus to come into his heart. So *my* hands were tied. I could do nothing to see that he received some nurturing and teaching— things that I believe are important for a baby Christian.

Well, the only thing I know to do in cases like this is pray, because God's hands are never tied! Oh, if we would only come to this, the most effective weapon we have, more quickly than we do! And so I began to pray intensely and fervently for the Lord to raise this man up and make him a mighty disciple. I prayed for the Lord to send someone into his life who was a Christian to teach and encourage him.

In stepped the Lord! Within a few days our new brother in Christ called me to ask me to pray some specific prayers with him. And he related an exciting bit of news to me. He is the manager of some condominiums that are owned by my husband, and a man from the Gideon Bible Society had come by with a box of Bibles for the condominiums. Our friend saw this as the hand of God in his life. He knew that the Lord was reaching out to him, and I saw it as an answer to prayer.

But I continued to pray. Within a few weeks, one Tuesday afternoon at 4:30 (I shall never forget it as long as I live), a young man who lives in Dallas called me on the telephone. I only knew this young man remotely. I had met him once or twice and knew very little about him. He said, with what appeared to be fear and trembling, "I need to talk to someone. I am confused. I have read your book *(Milk for Babes)* and I see that we have been through many of the same things. My wife is leaving me and I know that I don't want her to leave. I know that I need something, but I am not sure what it is. I'm confused about who Jesus Christ is. Can you tell me?" I asked him to come right over.

When he walked in the front door, this handsome young man looked like walking death. His face was ashen. His eyes were lifeless. There was no expression to be seen in his countenance. He sat down and began to tell me what had happened. It was a real horror story, but typical of so many people today. He was married to a beautiful young woman and had two precious young boys, five and eight. In his business he traveled a great deal and spent a lot of time away from home. In his business travels he had become quite involved with a young female "guru" of sorts in California, and he was playing around with all sorts of metaphysical religions and eastern philosophies. To say the least, he was mixed up. He later told me that as I began to tell him who Jesus Christ was to me, suddenly nothing else mattered any more. The Holy Spirit moved in his heart. He asked Jesus to come into his heart. This all happened only a matter of minutes from the time he entered the door. He wept deep, cleansing tears of repentance. The face of death disappeared before my very eyes. He rose to leave as suddenly as he had come, promising to bring his wife the following evening to the Bible study in our home.

That next evening he returned with a very angry, resentful wife in tow. She was fed up with him and the last thing she wanted to do was, as she put it, "help" him. But she came nevertheless. (The Lord brought her!) Before the evening was over, this young couple was committed to Jesus Christ, and filled with the Spirit. In addition, they made a new commitment to one another. The young man renounced, confessed, and was cleansed and delivered of all dealings in occult and cult activities. They are in several Bible studies a week, and guess what! This second young man is teaching our California friend what he is learning here in Dallas when he is in

California on business, which is frequently. He has also gotten our first friend in a church!

A most unusual and exciting answer to prayer, wouldn't you say? Now you tell me! Is that a great and mighty God we serve? It thrills my heart and keeps me praying, praising, and worshiping Him. These are only two of many, almost daily miracles that have occurred in my life and can occur in the life of any believer. It doesn't matter who you are. It is not you. It is God. God has worked through donkeys and through bushes. You don't have to be somebody in the eyes of the world to be somebody in the kingdom of God. And all it takes to be used of God is surrender and commitment to Him—commitment to study the Word, pray, praise, worship, listen, and obey. Every problem is an opportunity for God, and He is looking for committed people through whom He can work.

These two examples from my own testimony were meant to show you how the strength/praise of God flows out of the life of a believer—power that overcomes the enemy. The first example was victory over sickness and physical death. The second example was victory over the eternal damnation of three people. The devil quakes when we pray, praise, and worship. There is no more powerful combination! The power of God flows forth out of praise and worship.

The second spiritual principle I see in "the Lion of the tribe of Judah" is that praise overcomes our flesh. The lion is a carnivorous animal. He is a "flesh-eater." And remember that Judah means "praise to God." The Bible says that praise is a flesh-eater too.

PROVERBS 27:21: "As the fining pot for silver, and the furnace for gold; so is a man to his praise."

It's very interesting to me that praise consumes the very thing that restrains us from praise, and that is our own flesh. Even though we are new creatures in Christ, even though old things have passed away and all things are new (2 Cor. 5:17), even though we can come boldly before the throne of grace for mercy and grace to help in time of need (Heb. 4:16), we still have the old flesh (or carnality) that gets in our way. "Now then it is no more I that do it, but sin that dwelleth in me. For I know that in me (that is, in my **flesh,**) dwelleth no good thing . . ." (Rom. 7:17–18, parentheses not mine). "So then they that are in the flesh cannot please God" (Rom. 8:8). "For the flesh lusteth against the Spirit, and the Spirit against the flesh: and these are contrary the one to the other: so that ye cannot do the things that ye would" (Gal. 5:17).

Our flesh must be crucified, destroyed, rent—even as the veil in the temple was rent from top to bottom when Jesus died on the cross. There is a one-time, major "death" experience for our souls, much as we saw at the table of shewbread. However, it is also a daily process as well. Paul said, ". . . I die daily" (1 Cor. 15:31; see also Luke 9:23 and Phil. 3:10).

There are two interesting analogies about this daily process called "dying to self." The first compares the process to that of peeling an onion layer by layer. The Lord is gentle, tender and merciful with His children. He does not give us more than we can bear. He peels away one layer of our "flesh" at a time, or He may strip off several layers at once. Then He lets us rest for awhile. We could not bear it if we saw all of our human flaws at once.

The second analogy is that of refining gold. Raw ore is taken from the ground and melted down over intense heat. The dross begins to rise to the surface and is skimmed off the molten rock. This skimming is repeated until the final product is pure. It gleams and glistens. It is beautiful. I have heard it said that the Lord continues to skim and skim until He can see His reflection in us. Or at least He is working toward that end result.

For me, the major death experience took two years. It involved surrender of two major areas in my life, connected with two of the most important people in my life. I will share one of them with you. When I had been a Christian for two years, my twenty-year-old son had a nervous breakdown. In the early months of this sad time in all of our lives there was great concern that he might harm himself. The Christian counselors told me that I must give up my efforts to protect him and keep him alive. They told me that I must release him to God. Their reason for this was that it was only when he was free to choose to die that he would be free to choose to live. I recognized this fiery trial in my life as a great opportunity for God. Much as Abraham placed Isaac on the altar of sacrifice and was willing to give up his only son, I placed my son on the altar of God and said, "Not my will, but thine, O Lord. I trust you, Lord. I know it isn't your will that he kill himself, so I surrender him to you." I then dedicated myself to intercessory prayer in behalf of my son and the praise and worship of God to the best of my ability—much as Abraham did (Gen. 22:5) when he placed Isaac on the altar. I didn't do this perfectly. There have been rough moments, even difficult days and weeks over the last three years. But I continued to turn him over to the Lord. Every time I have taken him off of the altar, as soon as I find myself worried or fearful, I simply put him back in the hands of God. I hope I haven't made it sound easy, because it isn't. Surrender of problems such as these is a moment-by-moment walk of faith. Today my son is in school, making As and Bs. The Lord is still healing him, and to God be the glory! Not just for his healing but for the grace He has given me during those difficult times.

Another layer of surrender that I think is important to share with you has its roots in the same problem I shared with you earlier. Because I experienced so much rejection in my life, I had always cared very much what people thought of me. That didn't stop me from doing what I wanted to do before I knew the Lord, but I suffered from this problem severely. The more I rebelled and refused to conform, the more I suffered from the rejection. It was a vicious cycle.

Then when I became a Christian and began to share my new faith in Jesus, I was face to face with a different sort of nonconformity to the world. When I began to give my testimony, I was confronted by many unsaved friends and acquaintances who did not understand. Many of them ridiculed me. One lady was overheard to have said in a beauty parlor, "It will be interesting to see how long Clint will tolerate Anne and Jesus! He won't hang around that situation long!" Accepting this kind of rejection came pretty easily for me because I knew where the lady was coming from. I used to say the same sort of things about born-again Christians myself. I knew quickly as a new Christian that the lost do not and cannot understand spiritual things. I no longer cared what the world thought of my Christianity.

However, the next step for me was surrendering to the Lord my concern about what Christians thought of me. We have all unfortunately been confronted with the many differences we Christians have among ourselves. Within one year after I was born again, the Lord began to call me clearly to be conformed to Him and not to other Christians. To the best of my ability I have tried to walk in obedience to His leading. I have kept myself immersed in the Scriptures and have called upon the Lord to keep me from anything unscriptural. In the last three years, I have also had the blessed covering of a wonderful believing husband to whom I am submitted, and in the last fifteen months of a marvelous pastor, to whom Clint and I are both submitted. I go to the trouble to tell you this so you will know that I recognize my need for spiritual authority and leadership. I desire it and feel it is important that I have a spiritual covering.

And now I want to tell you what I have been leading up to. When I came into the Spirit-filled life and Davidic praise and worship, I had to surrender once again that desire to please everyone . . . only this time it was in the Christian community. Writing this book was a big commitment for me, because I have encountered many people in the body of Christ who do not see the validity and truth of extravagant Davidic praise and worship. I know people who are "turned off" by it, much as Michal was when she saw David leaping and playing and dancing before the Lord. And yet I believe with all my heart that many in the body of Christ would be receptive to such things if there were teaching from the Scriptures to open the eyes of their understanding. I cannot say no to God, regardless of what anyone says. I say this with humility and in the fear of the Lord, because I know that He tries and tests my attitudes and ways.

At a time when disapproval by people in the body was unusually severe and I was hurting deeply, I cried out to the Lord, "Jesus, I have so wanted to be obedient to you. I have, to the best of my ability, tried to be what I believed you wanted me to be and do what you wanted me to do. Now there are those who reject me or say I am in error. But Lord, I stand before you, deeply in love with you. If I am in error, change me." As clear as could be, that still, small voice spoke within me and said, "My child, are you going to walk the way I have called you to walk, or are you going to walk the way man wants you to walk?" Of course, my answer had to be, "Thy will be done in my life, Lord." From that moment on, I have walked in freedom from the burden of what people think. I know that no matter what I believe, no matter how much I break my back to do all that people ask me to do, there will be those who disagree with me, and there will always be those who say I am not doing enough. Therefore, I listen to the voice of the Lord and look to my spiritual authority, my husband.

There are further complications with the problems I have had with rejection. The current layer of my onion that the Lord is peeling away relates to the fact that Murchison is such a well-known name in the world and consequently also well known in the Christian realm. Because I find myself receiving much attention and recognition, this encourages fleshly thoughts in me. Public acclaim is addictive, and it is something the Lord has quickened to me to watch for in myself, for His Word says, "Casting all your care upon him; for he careth for you. Be sober, be vigilant; because your adversary the devil, as a roaring lion, walketh about, seeking whom he may devour: Whom resist stedfast in the faith, knowing that the same afflictions are accomplished in your brethren that are in the world" (1 Pet. 5:7–9).

This temptation to be noticed is an ungodly one, and when those fiery darts begin to fly at me and imaginations and high things begin to exalt themselves against the knowledge of God through my thoughts, I first repent and ask for forgiveness and cleansing. Then I take those thoughts captive to the obedience of Christ (2 Cor. 10:5). When I have sudden desires to be noticed in a crowd, I am committed to bringing that ungodly desire into line with the Word of God. I resist the temptation just as Jesus did in the wilderness. I wield the sword of the Spirit. I stand on Scripture. I say to the devil, "It is written!" Then whatever scripture the Lord brings to my memory, I stand firmly on it. And I enter into praise to God, for Scripture says, "Let the high praises of God be in their mouth, and a twoedged sword in their hand" (Ps. 149:6). It takes both! It's interesting, isn't it, that praise not only brings "flesh" to the light, it also overcomes it!

And I do not resist the chastening of the Lord, for His chastening is meant to make me a "partaker of His holiness" and it "yieldeth the peaceable fruit of righteousness unto them which are exercised thereby" (Heb. 12:10, 11). I count all trials as joy, knowing that the testing of my faith brings patience and when patience has its perfect work, I will lack nothing (James 1:2–4). And I "greatly rejoice . . . in heaviness through manifold temptations: That the trial of (my) faith, being much more precious than of gold that perisheth, though it be tried with fire, might be found unto praise and honour and glory at the appearing of Jesus Christ" (1 Pet. 1:6–7).

We can take ten years to learn one year's lesson, or we can take one year to learn ten years' lessons. This all depends on the attitude of the individual believer during testing. We can either walk forward through the valleys, in faith and confidence and with a glad heart, or we can be dragged through it heels first. If we choose this latter course, it is not likely that we will ever walk in the fullness of all that God intends for us.

My dear friend, I open myself up to you in the hope that it will strengthen you. God is certainly dealing with this problem in my life and I am so thankful to Him. It is not pleasant, but I want Him to deal with it. I invite Him to nail this flesh to the cross, for anything that is not of God in me keeps my relationship with Him from flourishing, and that relationship is all that matters to me in life. No price is too high. I thank God through Jesus Christ, our Lord, that He shall deliver me from the power of sin and flesh.

Surrender (dying to self) is giving up control of the problems of our lives, such as the problem with my son. It is also giving up control of the work the Lord wants to do in our lives. How often I have heard people tragically say, "I'll do anything you want, Lord, but . . .!" "I'm your servant, God, only don't make me . . .!" "What would my parents, husband, children, pastor think if I . . .!" How the Lord longs to hear us, His children, say, "Anything you say, Lord!"

God is holy. He cannot look upon sin (Hab. 1:13). Even though we are the righteousness of Christ and God sees us as righteous, we are continually in the process of being conformed to the image of God. That means that there must be a "dying to self."

When we are confronted with the manifested presence of the Holy God in Davidic praise and worship, we are suddenly grossly aware of our depravity and perversity. Isaiah responded, "Woe is me! For I am undone; because I am a man of unclean lips, and I dwell in the midst of a people of unclean lips: for mine eyes have seen the King, the Lord of hosts" (Isa. 6:5). Moses said, "O my Lord, I am not eloquent, neither heretofore, nor since thou hast spoken unto thy servant: but I am slow of speech, and of a slow tongue" (Exod. 4:10). Job said, "Behold, I am vile; what shall I answer thee? I will lay mine hand upon my mouth" (40:4). Jeremiah cried unto the Lord, "Ah, Lord God! behold, I cannot speak: for I am a child" (1:6).

All of our inadequacies and imperfections rise to our consciousness in the presence of the Almighty God. Sins are no longer relative. To the soul of the person who walks in close communion with the Lord, even the very smallest act of unfaithfulness becomes great. A sin which is not even noticed or which is regarded as trivial to some would appear to be a heinous crime to the believer abiding in the manifested presence of God. Others who are not so far along on their Christian walks may be content with being kept from what is considered gross sin, but the believer with a mature heart of integrity seeks to walk in unbroken communion with Him and cannot excuse in himself the smallest act of disobedience or insensitivity to God's will. This is the price we pay for intimate fellowship with God. But no matter how painful the price, it is nothing compared to the joy and blessing of worship to the Almighty and Living God. The unpleasantness of seeing ourselves as we really are is eased by the grace of God through His forgiveness and cleansing power. When the Lord reveals these areas in me with which He wishes to deal, I merely bring them to the cross and ask Him to nail them there.

This seems so clear to me, but let's say it one more time. We are able to see the manifested glory of God in praise and worship to the degree that our flesh has been crucified. As we draw nearer to God through praise and worship, one of the natural results of such intimate fellowship is the intense refining which brings about more of this dying to our flesh, which brings us under greater submission to the control of the Holy Spirit. The searing light of the Shekinah glory is keener than any laser beam and will reveal any hidden darkness (unholiness) within, "for our God is a consuming fire" (Heb. 12:29).

The last of the three spiritual principles I see in "the Lion of the tribe of Judah," is the result of the first two. It is an outflowing of the rivers of living waters in our lives (John 7:37–39). Ezekiel 47 gives us a beautiful picture of those rivers of living waters. They begin with a trickle. This represents the new believer and the carnal believer. Then the waters are ankle deep. This is symbolic of the believer as he begins to walk in the Spirit. Next the waters have risen to the knees. This reflects our prayer-, praise-, and worship-life. Then the waters are up to the loins. Reference to the loins in Scriptures always has to do with fruitfulness in the life of the believer and vigor and power in service for the Lord. Finally the believer finds himself in waters that cannot be passed over, and he is swimming in the refreshing, living waters of the Holy Spirit of God. He is lost in Jesus, consecrated totally to Him.

The result in the life of the believer who finds himself swimming in these waters is that ". . . every thing that liveth, which moveth, whithersoever the rivers shall come, shall live: and there shall be a very great multitude of fish (Jesus said in Matt. 4:19, 'I will make you fishers of men'), because these waters shall come thither: for they shall be healed ('they will lay hands on the sick, and they will recover'—Mark 16:18); and every thing shall live whither the river cometh. . . . And by the river upon the bank thereof, on this side and on that side, shall grow all trees for meat, whose leaf shall not fade, neither shall the fruit thereof be consumed ('My God shall supply all my needs according to his riches in glory in Christ Jesus'—Phil. 4:19): it shall bring forth new fruit according to his months, because their waters they issued out of the sanctuary ('They that wait upon the Lord shall renew their strength; they shall mount up with wings like eagles; they shall run, and not be weary; and they shall walk, and not faint'—Isa. 40:31): and the fruit thereof shall be for meat, and its leaf thereof for medicine" (Ezek. 47:9, 12).

Here we have a perfect picture of the rest of God. We see most of the aspects of being a Christian, and they are all accomplished by the river and not the believer. Isaiah 33:21 says that this river is a place of rest and a place of safety. "But there the glorious Lord will be unto us a place of broad rivers and streams; wherein shall go **no** galley with oars (rest), neither shall gallant ship (enemy or foe) pass thereby (safety)."

This is a spiritual picture of the life of a believer that is surrendered, tried, and tested. It is the result of Davidic praise and worship and meditating day and night in the Word of God (Ps. 1:1–3). These are key elements to this quality of life for the believer.

Out of a heart of integrity flows our prayer life, meditation in the Scriptures, and Davidic praise and worship, and the glory and power of God are manifested in our lives. This equips us for anything that God requires of us. It equips us to be His instruments. Our first ministry is to God, and out of that ministry flows the power of God that equips us for the other two categories of ministry in Scripture—ministry to the body of Christ and ministry to the lost. (Using the pattern of the tabernacle of Moses, we can see clearly that the ministry to the lost and to baby Christians is in the Outer Court, the ministry to the body of Christ is in the Holy Place and the ministry to God is in the Holy of Holies.)

I hope you can see from the examples I have given in my own personal life, which is far from perfect, that when we have a heart of integrity, then our priorities are in the right order, and all things fall into place. I don't have to go out and look for people to witness to. The Lord brings them to me, wherever I am. It doesn't matter whether I know anyone or whether anyone knows me. The Lord does it and He then gets all the glory for it.

Let us forget what lies behind, dear friend, and reach forward to what lies ahead. Let us press on toward the goal for the prize of the upward call of God in Christ Jesus (Phil. 3:13–14).

JOHN 15:7: "If ye abide in me, and my words *(rhēma)* abide in you, ye shall ask what ye will, and it shall be done unto you."

ISAIAH 61:1–3: "The Spirit of the Lord God is upon me; because the Lord hath anointed me to preach good tidings unto the meek; he hath sent me to bind up the brokenhearted, to proclaim liberty to the captives, and the opening of the prison to them that are bound; To proclaim the acceptable year of the Lord, and the day of vengeance of our God; to comfort all that mourn; To appoint unto them that mourn in Zion, to give unto them beauty for ashes, the oil of joy for mourning, the garment of praise for the spirit of heaviness; that they might be called trees of righteousness, the planting of the Lord, that he might be glorified."

PSALM 40:2–3: "He brought me up also out of an horrible pit, out of the miry clay, and set my feet upon a rock, and established my goings. And he hath put a new song in my mouth, even praise unto our God: many shall see it, and fear, and shall trust in the Lord."

PSALM 46:4: "There is a river, the streams whereof shall make glad the city of God, the holy place of the tabernacles of the Most High."

Father, we come to You in great humility, recognizing all too well how frail we really are. We thank You for Jesus, who once walked in this fallen world. We thank You that He took all of our frailties and sins to the cross and died in our place. We thank You that we are hidden in Him. We humbly confess that we are weak and have flaws and we seek your strength, for your Word says, "in my weakness I will be made strong in Christ Jesus." We thank You that we can know You, Jesus, and the power of your resurrection and the fellowship of your sufferings and can be conformed to your death. Help us, Lord. Give us the courage to press on . . . to walk in all the spiritual truths of Davidic praise and worship and the Lion of the tribe of Judah . . . to surrender all that is ours to You that You might raise us up in that resurrection power and we might swim in the rivers of living waters . . . that we might overcome all the power of the enemy . . . and that we might be endued with that power from on high . . . power that enables us to minister in praise and worship to You . . . power that enables us to minister to our brothers and sisters in Christ . . . and power that enables us to minister to the lost and dying of the world. Overcome our flesh, Lord, and make overcomers out of us in this world. It is for your glory and in your name that we pray. Amen.

A Royal Priesthood

1 PETER 2:9: "But ye are a chosen generation, a royal priesthood, a holy nation, a peculiar people; that ye should shew forth the praises of him who hath called you out of darkness into his marvelous light."

There are many wonderful truths in this verse of scripture, but the one I want to examine in this chapter is the role of the royal priesthood. I find it interesting that this verse says we are (present tense) a royal priesthood. Yet as Christians, we know very little about this role to God. You and I have seen in a very limited way through the study of Moses' tabernacle earlier what that role is, but I thought it might help to see what the Bible has to say on the subject.

Under the Old Covenant, the Lord chose the tribe of Levi to be His priests (Deut. 10:8–9). Even among the tribe of priests, there was only one High Priest, and he and only he could enter into the Holy of Holies to make atonement for the sins of the people once a year (Heb. 9:6–7). This High Priest was a type of Jesus, our great High Priest, who was to come (Heb. 4:14–15). By His death and resurrection, He opened the way into the Holy of Holies for us, His royal priesthood of the New Covenant (Heb. 10:19–22, 4:16). And yet few of us understand our role as priests to the most high God.

I mentioned earlier that the tabernacle of Moses gives us the clear priority of the ministry of the priest. The ministry in the

Holy of Holies is the ministry to God. That is our number one priority. The ministry in the Holy Place is the ministry to believers. That is our second priority. And the ministry in the outer court is to the lost of the world and the newly saved. That is our third priority. When I mentioned this to one friend, his response was, "Yes, but Christ gave the great commission. He told us to go into all the world and teach the gospel." And I believe in the importance of the great commission. It was a command of Jesus, and I am doing my part to the best of my ability. However, Jesus was talking to worshipers; we saw that earlier in Luke 24:49–53. In only a casual perusal of the Book of Acts, you will discover that the first-century church was a praising, worshiping church. The Epistles of the New Testament were all written for building up of the body of Christ. So we can see that there was strong evidence of all three ministries in the early church. However, today it seems that many of us think there is only one ministry and that is to the lost and to the baby Christian.

Once again I would like to quote Tozer's priceless little booklet on worship: "We're here to be worshipers **first** and workers only second. We take a convert and immediately make a worker out of him. God never meant it to be so. God meant that a convert should learn to be a worshiper, and after that he can learn to be a worker."

I have tried to leave room for other viewpoints throughout this book, and yet I do not think I can finish it without saying one or two things which may draw disagreement but which seem very clear to me. In my opinion, many Christians do not have a full understanding of ministry to the body, for I see and know lots of people who go to church hurting and who leave hurting. Nor do they have an understanding of the ministry to God. Our concept of praise and worship is so very far removed from the Scriptures.

And I believe also that we have all placed far too much emphasis on learning and not enough emphasis on experience of truth in our lives. As it says in Timothy, we have a form of godliness, but we deny the power. We are ever learning and never able to come to the knowledge of the truth (2 Tim. 3:5, 7). We have allowed pet doctrines, religious traditions, good works, possessions, seminars, tapes, books and pride ("I'm right!"—or concern with what others think of us), to become idols in our lives. These subtle forms of idolatry often "look" good but estrange us from God, and, of course, restrain us from complete devotion and dedication to the walk of a heart of integrity toward God. Idolatry restrains us from doing His will in all things.

I would like to take a quick look at what the Scriptures say about idolatry.

EZEKIEL 14:4–5: "Therefore speak unto them, and say unto them, Thus saith the Lord God; Every man of the house of Israel that setteth up his idols in his heart, and putteth the stumblingblock of his iniquity before his face . . . they are all estranged from me through their idols."

2 KINGS 17:41: "So these nations feared the Lord, and **(also)** served their graven images . . ."

JEREMIAH 2:13: "For my people have committed two evils; they have **forsaken me the fountain of living waters, and hewed out cisterns, broken cisterns, that can hold no water.**"

Having read these scriptures over a few times, I would like to tell you what they say to me. They say to me first that an idol does not always have to be something made with our hands. It can be something in our hearts. Second I see that this idolatry of heart estranges us from God. Next I see that a person can be a believer and still serve graven images. And last, I see that these idols are of absolutely no purpose but destruction in our lives. Tying the above scriptures in with the following one will give us a clear picture of much of the church today:

EZEKIEL 44:10–16: "And the Levites (the priests) that are gone away far from me, when Israel went astray, which went astray away from me **after their idols;** they shall even bear their iniquity. **Yet they shall be ministers in my sanctuary,** having charge at the gates of the house, and ministering to the house: they shall slay the burnt offering and the sacrifice for the people, and they shall stand before them **to minister unto them.** Because they ministered unto them before their idols, and caused the house of Israel to fall into iniquity; therefore have I lifted up mine hand against them, saith the Lord God, and they shall bear their iniquity (broken fellowship). **And they shall not come near unto me, to do the office of a priest unto me, nor to come near to any of my holy things, in the most holy place:** but they shall bear their shame, and their abominations which they have committed. But I will make them **keepers of the charge of the house, for all the service thereof, and for all that shall be done in it.** But the priests, the Levites, the sons of Zadok, who kept the charge of my sanctuary when the children of Israel went astray from me, **they shall come near to me to minister unto me, and they shall stand before me** to offer unto me the fat and the blood, saith the Lord God. They shall enter into my sanctuary, and they shall come near to my table, to minister **unto me,** and they shall keep my charge."

In spite of these idols, God will still allow His people to continue to serve. We can evangelize, teach, preach, pray for the sick and see them healed, visit those in prisons, intercede in behalf of kings and nations, and we will see results even with unconfessed, hidden sin in our lives. After all, God has spoken through a donkey and a bush! God will honor many of our labors. But the Word of God says He will not allow us in the Holy of Holies. He will not allow us in His Presence to minister to Him.

From my own personal life I have seen that I have given my testimony all over and many have been saved. I have given my tithes and offerings. I have worked on Christian projects. I have prayed . . . a lot! And I have seen many answers to my prayers. But once I started worshiping the Lord, He began to reveal many areas of sin in my life of which I had no awareness. The presence of the Lord brings hidden things to the light. Once we become worshipers, then we become supersensitive to sin in our lives.

The choice is ours to make. We can remain in the outer court like the priests in Ezekiel 44:10–14, or we can set our face like a flint to enter into the ministry of the royal priesthood . . . to minister to God first!

In closing this chapter on the royal priesthood, I think it is essential to return to the opening verse, for in that verse it states the purpose of the priesthood. "But ye are a chosen generation, a **royal priesthood,** an holy nation, a peculiar people; **that ye should shew forth the praises of him** who hath called you out of darkness into his marvelous light" (1 Pet. 2:9). In *God's Best Secrets* Andrew Murray says of this verse, "The glory of heaven is the worship of the Lamb and of Him that sitteth on the Throne. If we take part with all our hearts in the Song of the Lamb, we shall realize that we are priests of the Throne of Grace. As priests we worship God and the Lamb, and with hearts full of adoration may approach the Throne of the Lamb for ourselves and others. As kings we receive the abundance of grace that we may reign in life, over sin and the power of the world, so that we may bring liberty to the captives. Such an overcoming life on earth will form and prepare us for sitting with Christ on His Throne."

Praise is our first ministry! And it truly sets us apart as a peculiar people!

Lord God, Creator of the universe, what a privilege we have to enter into your throne room, to stand in your presence, to have your wisdom and your beauty and your love wash over us. Lord, help us to enter into our role as priest and minister to You. Cleanse us from sin. We have allowed idols in our hearts. We have been lazy and allowed others to do our thinking and formulating, when there was available to us the mind of Christ. Help us to grow, Lord Jesus. We pray fervently and reach out to You, Holy Spirit, our teacher. Teach us. Lead us. In Jesus' name we pray. Amen.

The Remnant within the Remnant
(within the Remnant
within the Remnant)

As I have studied through the Bible, I have become more and more aware that it describes believers of two to four kinds. There are those who walk after the flesh and allow the cares of the world to take precedence in their lives, and there are those who walk in the Spirit with a heart of integrity toward God. And the Bible also reveals that with further subdivisions in those two groups, there are four types of believers. This chapter briefly studies both groups.

Digging for insights about the two—the remnant within the remnant—and the four—the remnant within the remnant within the remnant within the remnant—has brought me invaluable rewards in my study of the Word of God and of the body of Christ. Obviously, a volume could be written on this subject, but I believe the Lord can use even a cursory glance at it to enrich our understanding.

There is no clearer picture in the Bible of the two-part remnant than what happened to Israel after the death of David. This nation, once specially chosen by God, was split into two kingdoms, Israel and Judah. Israel became lukewarm in its commitment to God, but Judah kept on in the same commitment to obedience and praise and worship that David had. It continued to live up to the meaning of its name, "praise to God." But let's return to the beginning, to the birth of Israel as a nation.

The History

When God's people, Israel, departed from Egypt and crossed through the Red Sea, they were a nation called unto God.

DEUTERONOMY 26:18–19: "And the Lord hath avouched thee this day to be his peculiar people, as he hath promised thee, and that thou shouldest keep all his commandments; And to make thee high above all nations which he hath made, in praise, and in name, and in honour; and that thou mayest be an holy people unto the Lord thy God, as he hath spoken."

And even though this nation Israel complained and murmured against God, they were His people.

NUMBERS 23:19–21: "God is not a man, that he should lie; neither the son of man, that he should repent: hath he said, and shall he not do it? or hath he spoken, and shall he not make it good? Behold, I have received commandment to bless: and he hath blessed: and I cannot reverse it. He hath not beheld iniquity in Jacob, neither hath he seen perverseness in Israel; the Lord his God is with him, and the shout of a king is among them."

But the remnant of believers began to separate and be refined as pure gold. There has never been more than a remnant of people who believed in the true and living God in the whole world, and Israel at that time was it. All whom death "passed over" in Egypt were saved from the enemy by the blood of the sacrificial lamb (Exod. 12:13). They were believers under the Old Covenant. All were baptized in sea and cloud (1 Cor. 10:2), and yet God separated the remnant out after forty years in the wilderness. All those over twenty years of age, except Joshua and Caleb, were left to die in the wilderness because of their disobedience and rebellion, including Moses. They were not allowed to enter into the promised land (Num. 32:10–13). It isn't that they were eternally damned; they just didn't enter into the rest of salvation (Heb. 3:19).

Once that first remnant crossed over into the promised land, they began to take possession of it. As they gained possession, even this remnant disobeyed God in that they did not completely drive out all the inhabitants of the land and destroy their idols as He had commanded them to do (Num. 33:51–55). His patience was sorely tested (Judg. 1:27–2:3), especially as even the priests were leading ungodly lives (1 Sam. 2:22–34). The people of Israel began to clamor for a king to rule over them, preferring someone they could see and touch to the Living God who dwelt in their midst (1 Sam. 8:5–8). So God chose Saul to rule over them (1 Sam. 9:16–17). But Saul himself fell into rebellion and disfavor (1 Sam. 13:3–14), and the Lord chose David to be the king (1 Sam. 16:1, 12–13). David, who was of the tribe of Judah (1 Sam. 17:12), was considered by God to be a "man after His own heart" (Acts 13:22). In spite of sin with Bath-sheba, David's reign as king was the second most important in the history of Israel, because it was with David that God covenanted the eternal throne upon which the Messiah, Jesus Christ, the King of Kings, would reign forever (2 Sam. 7:16. Of course, the most important king is Jesus!) It was through the line of David and the tribe of Judah that the Lion of the tribe of Judah (Jesus!) was manifested in the flesh (Matt. 1:1–16 and Rev. 5:5).

David was king over all Israel, but after he died, his son by Bath-sheba, Solomon, became king (1 Kings 2:10–12). He took as his wives many heathen women who brought their idols into the temple of God, and the judgment of God promised a severe split in the remnant of Israel again (1 Kings 11:1–13). When Solomon died, his son, Rehoboam, ruled over all Israel. But just as the Lord had sworn, Israel was divided into two separate nations, Israel and Judah. "And none but the tribe of Judah followed after the house of David" (1 Kings 12:16–20).

The above brief scan through this period of Bible history leaves me in no doubt that the "hot" remnant was continually in a state of being separated out from the "lukewarm" and the "cold." The point to be shared here is that truth does that. Truth divides, and divides, and divides, and divides.

JOHN 17:17: "Sanctify them through thy truth: thy word is truth."

God's word is truth, and it does separate its faithful followers out to God to greater and greater degrees. The word *sanctify* used in this verse is *hagiazō*, and it means, according to *An Expository Dictionary of New Testament Words* by W. E. Vine, "the setting apart (separation) of the believer for God . . . the separation of the believer from the world in his behaviour, by the Father through the Word." We see this further illuminated in the following scripture.

HEBREWS 4:12: "For the word of God is quick, and powerful, and sharper than any two-edged sword, piercing even to the dividing asunder of soul and spirit, and of the joints and marrow, and is a discerner of the thoughts and intents of the heart."

Dividing as used in Hebrews 4:12 in Greek is *měrismŏs*, and it means "a separation or distribution; dividing asunder; gift."

As each new spiritual truth becomes an experiential part of our lives, we are separated a little more from the world. Spiritual truth **does** separate us from our unsaved and carnal friends first, and also from those who do not choose to walk in the truth as it is revealed to them. To a certain extent that is true also with those who have not had revealed to them those same truths which have been revealed to you and in which you are walking.

I felt this kind of separation when a friend of mine called me the other day to invite me to go to a movie. She is a "backslidden" Christian friend of many years who has recently rededicated her life to Jesus Christ. When she called, I was deeply involved in studying and preparing for writing this book. I feel that the Lord quite some time ago set me apart from secular forms of entertainment such as movies, night clubs, television, radio, music, and to a large degree nice ladies' luncheons, with the one exception of my husband's business entertainment. The Lord not only showed me what a waste of time most of these sorts of activities were for me and not only removed every desire for such things from my life, but He also showed me how much of it poisoned me spiritually.

When I told my friend this, I could tell by her response that she thought I was being fanatical about it. I said it with as much love as I could and explained to her that it was my choice for me and that I was in no way laying my Christian walk and responsibility on her. We are all in different places in our spiritual growth. We must walk our walk as God has called us and leave others free to walk the walk God has given them. We so often try to squeeze others into the mold of our theology or our personal spiritual opinions and growth. It seems to me the Lord simply does not operate that way, and we shouldn't either. The Lord gave the Holy Spirit for that purpose. We are to encourage one another to walk in obedience and pray that we will, but each walk is unique, as each child is unique. And our encouragement is to be given with much gentleness, love, and sensitivity to the Holy Spirit.

I did not expect this sister to walk the way God is leading me, because He has not done that work in her heart. I told her that I would be delighted to have her come to Bible study, to prayer group or to a private lunch with me, but that I would not enjoy going to a movie. She and I have delightful fellowship when we spend time together.

In this chapter we have been looking at how truth separates, at how it separated Israel out from the world into a remnant of believers and then how it further separated Judah/praise to God out from Israel into a remnant **within** the remnant. Now I would like to take this study even further.

Judah/Praise to God—The Faithful Remnant within the Remnant

All through the Psalms, we see that Israel was loved by God but that Judah, like David, was a people after God's own heart, who fulfilled **all** His will.

PSALM 114:2: "Judah (praise to God) was his sanctuary (dwelling place), and Israel his dominion."
PSALM 76:1: "In Judah (praise to God) is God **known:** his name is great in Israel."

The difference between Judah and Israel seems clear: God's

dominion (or realm, kingdom) is Israel and is symbolic, I believe, of the entire body of Christ. His sanctuary (dwelling place) is in Judah/praise to God. If you will recall, Psalm 22:3 says that God's dwelling place is praise, and the Hebrew word *nâvâh* means dwelling place/celebration of praise. And interestingly, the word *sanctuary*, used in Psalm 114:2 above, comes from the root word that means "sanctified" or "separated out." So this speaks to me of a dwelling place that is separated out to God, and the Bible says this sanctified place (sanctuary) is Judah/praise to God.

In Psalm 76:1, God's name is great in Israel, but he is **known** in Judah/praise to God. Christians are the people of His kingdom today, and He has dominion over all of us. His name is great to all of us, but He is **known** by, in, and through Judah/ praise to God.

This study of the remnant within the remnant can be taken further when we see that Jerusalem was the holy city, but that it was on Mount Zion, the holy mountain in the City of Jerusalem, that God dwelled. Zion is the City of David (1 Kings 8:1), and Zion is the place to which David brought the Ark of the Covenant out of captivity. Zion is the mount of which the Word of God speaks so tenderly (just as tenderly as it does of Judah/praise to God) and to which Jesus will return as the King of Kings and Lord of Lords.

PSALM 50:2: "Out of Zion, the perfection of beauty, God hath shined."
PSALM 76:2: "In Salem (Jerusalem) also is his tabernacle, and his dwelling place in Zion."
PSALM 87: "His foundation is in the holy mountains. The Lord loveth the gates of Zion more than all the dwellings of Jacob (Israel). Glorious things are spoken of thee, O city of God. Selah. . . . And of Zion it shall be said, This and that man was born in her: and the highest himself shall establish her. The Lord shall count, when he writeth up the people, that this man was born there. Selah. As well the singers as the players on instruments shall be there: all my springs are in thee."
OBADIAH 17: ". . . upon Mount Zion shall be deliverance, and there shall be holiness. . . ."

The Christian is spiritual Zion. We are spiritually born into Zion. . . .

HEBREWS 12:22: ". . . ye (believers) are come unto Mount Sion, and unto the city of the living God, the heavenly Jerusalem, and to an innumerable company of angels."

Yes, we have been born again into Zion (Ps. 87:5–6), and through the blood of Jesus we have been born again into the tribe of Judah/praise to God. But don't we desire more than the birth? Don't we desire to go on to spiritual maturity? Don't we desire to be seen by God as David was seen, as men after His own heart, who fulfill **all his** will? Don't we desire to walk in the kingdom of God now, in all the fullness of God (Eph. 3:19)? Don't we desire the reality in our lives of the heavenly Jerusalem and the innumerable company of angels? Don't we want to be a part of the restoration of the tabernacle of David? I do! "For the Lord hath chosen Zion; he hath desired it for his habitation. This is my rest for ever; here will I dwell; for I have desired it" (Ps. 132:13–14). "Praise *(t'hillâh)* waiteth for thee, O God, in Sion: and unto thee shall the vow be performed" (Ps. 65:1).

Even the casual reader of the Old Testament knows that Judah fell into darkness. And we have studied how the New Testament church had the same experience. But Malachi 3:4 promised, "Then shall the offering of Judah (praise to God) and Jerusalem be pleasant unto the Lord, as in the days of old, and as in former years." God is stirring up His people to Davidic praise and worship all over the world today. He is rebuilding the tabernacle of David upon spiritual Mount Zion. There is more, much more to being a Christian than witnessing, preaching, teaching, healing, going to church on Sunday, paying tithes, etc. Andrew Murray says it well in his devotional book, *God's Best Secrets:* "On the day of Pentecost a new dispensation of God came forth. **On God's part** it was the operation of the Holy Spirit in gifts and graces upon the whole church. **On man's part,** it was the adoration of God in spirit and in truth."

The fullest inheritance of a believer in Jesus Christ is that intense, intimate fellowship and communion with the Father that Jesus exemplified for us. Are we a part? For our Lord Jesus said, "But the hour cometh, and now is, when the true worshippers shall worship the Father in spirit and in truth: for the Father seeketh such to worship him. God is a Spirit: and they that worship him must worship him in spirit and in truth" (John 4:23–24).

PSALM 149:2: "Let Israel rejoice *(sâmach:* 'be glad, make merry') in him that made him: let the children of Zion be joyful *(gûwl:* 'Spin around in violent emotion') in their King."

JOEL 3:20: "But Judah (praise to God) shall dwell for ever, and Jerusalem from generation to generation."

JOEL 3:18: ". . . all the rivers of Judah (praise to God) shall flow with waters, and a fountain shall come forth of the house of the Lord, and shall water the valley. . . ."

The Remnant within the Remnant within the Remnant within the Remnant

Let us now move on to look briefly at four types of believers illustrated over and over in the Word of God. The first example I would like to use is from Exodus and concerns Moses and Mount Sinai. Four levels of believers are clearly delineated in their approach to the Mount. There were, of course, first the multitudes who were forbidden by God to come up to the Mount because of their fear, disobedience, and murmuring (Exod. 19:18–25, 20:18–19). The second group consisted of Moses, Aaron, Nadab and Abihu and seventy of the elders of Israel. They were allowed by God to come up on the mountain, but only a certain distance. In God's words, "You shall worship at a distance" (Exod. 24:1–11). At the third level, Joshua and Moses left the second group and moved higher up the mountain (Exod. 24:12–13). And the fourth level reveals Moses alone entering the midst of the cloud that covered the glory of the Lord atop the Mount (Exod. 24:18).

The second example that stands out in my mind involves Gideon and his soldiers. Here again we see the Lord separating out the remnants. First, there are the thirty-two thousand of the tribes of Manasseh, Asher, Zebulun and Naphtali (Judg. 6:35, 7:3). Second, there are the ten thousand (Judg. 7:3). Third, there are the three hundred (Judg. 7:7). And, of course, fourth, there was Gideon, who was called a "mighty man of valour" by the angel of the Lord (Judg. 6:12). It was Gideon to whom the Lord entrusted the responsibility of implicitly following His orders to go into battle against the Amalekites, Midianites, and the "children of the east," so that Israel might once again be delivered from bondage (Judg. 6–8:23). The Lord had once entrusted a very similar task to Moses in delivering Israel out of Egypt.

And the last example I want to share is one that involves followers of our Lord Jesus Himself. The first group was the seventy whom Jesus sent out two by two (Luke 10:1). The second was the twelve disciples (Luke 6:13). The third was the three—John, Peter and James—who went with Jesus up to the mountain where Jesus was transfigured before them (Matt. 17:1–2). And the fourth was John, "the disciple whom Jesus loved" (John 21:20). This was the disciple who reclined on the breast of Jesus at the last supper (John 13:23). This was the disciple to whom Jesus gave His great Revelation.

It seems apparent to me through the study of the three examples above and the study of the tabernacle of Moses earlier that our proximity to God is determined by our individual desire and faithfulness to respond to God's leading. Elsewhere I have referred to this as integrity of heart. The choice is ours, not God's. We choose to seek after God with all our heart, mind, soul, and strength. He then brings our integrity of heart to fruition, through our willing and faithful obedience. This requires as much surrender as we are able to give with each step that we take. It also requires an understanding of God's grace, for we can do nothing of ourselves. Paul understood this. He said, "I can do all things (that is, all things God asks of me individually) through Christ which strengtheneth me" (Phil. 4:13).

In my own life, the way I try to live this out is to continually tell the Lord that I want this with all my heart but that I can't do it without Him. As I trip and fall along the way, I call upon the Lord. I ask His forgiveness and cleansing. I receive it by faith.

He then picks me up and I proceed, beginning the process anew. We are not only born again by grace through faith, but we also live our entire Christian life by grace through faith.

Therefore, let us press on to "the mark for the prize of the high calling of God in Christ Jesus" (Phil. 3:14). How marvelous those words are to me!

Heavenly Father, our hearts are bursting forth in praise and worship and adoration of You. You are a mighty God. You are the Lord of Lords. You are the King of all Kings. Separate us out unto Yourself, Lord. Fill us to overflowing with desire for You and You alone. We draw near to You, Lord. Draw near to us. Give us the strength to walk in obedience to all your truth. Help us not to pick and choose but to be led by the Holy Spirit of God. Fill our hearts and mouths with praise and worship of You, O God. It is for your sake and in Jesus' name that we pray. Amen.

A Few Words of Encouragement
Before Closing

If you have never participated in praise and worship, I would like to share a few words of encouragement with you. As you come to the Lord to enter into this new and possibly strange ministry, come knowing that all you need is a willing heart. God will enable you. I say this especially for those who have had no teaching on the subject or who have had negative responses to praise and worship. When we have not been taught truth, such as Davidic praise and worship when it is clearly in the Bible, there will be a period of adjustment as we learn about it. I never had any negative teachings on the subject but I am acquainted with many people who have, and they tell me that it is very difficult to change their perceptions. There are feelings of bewilderment and confusion. Come to the Lord with these feelings. Press in to God. He will lead you and comfort you. "Joy cometh in the morning" (Ps. 30:5).

If you are mired in a pit of emotions and have never found the proper place to give of yourself emotionally, praise and worship are the vehicles necessary in your life. If you have been locked into a prison without access to feelings and emotions, praise and worship are the vehicles necessary for liberty in this area of your life. There is no love life that flourishes without feeling and emotion. There is no pleasure that can be fully enjoyed without giving expression to it. Praise and worship will not only open up your relationship with God. It will enable you to express yourself and your love to others more readily, and it will open up a greater sense of enjoyment in all things as well. We all need to love and to be loved.

For those who think they cannot sing, and for those who really cannot sing, the Word of God says, "Make a joyful noise unto the Lord." We praise and worship in obedience to a spiritual principle that is eternal. We do not do it to please ourselves or others. We do it to please God and therefore fulfill ourselves. When one becomes lost in the wonder of God, one is no longer aware of fleshly inadequacies but is focused upon the majesty and wonder of God. That is where our focus belongs.

Also, one thing I have noticed in my devotional times. With the Lord there is very definitely no set way to do anything. As soon as I find myself following a "pattern," I reach a dry place. The level of my praise and worship is not always the same either. Our hearts must be open to follow as the Holy Spirit leads, otherwise we are moving in our own flesh.

Sometimes I lie quietly bowed down before Him, waiting on Him to move me. Other times I stand with uplifted hands, eyes cast toward heaven. Sometimes I sing loudly and extravagantly, clapping, dancing and laughing, and often I sing gentle love songs to Him. But whatever form my expression takes, it is always in obedience to His leading and in His power. That way I stay open and my heart is fresh before Him. That way I am totally dependent upon Him for every step of the way.

Most of us come to dry times in our devotional lives and we may have quite different ways of dealing with them—reading, meditation, nature walks, prayer. I believe praise and worship are another all-important way. At one particularly dry time in my devotional life, I prayed and prayed that if there were unconfessed sin in my life that God would reveal it so that I could confess it, be cleansed and enter into worship in spirit and in truth. As I lay before Him, I distinctly heard the Lord say to me in that still but familiar small voice, "If every day were a mountaintop experience with me, you would become prideful and begin to think that **you** were doing it. I allow these dry places occasionally to keep you totally dependent upon me and to let you know that it is I and not you who gives life." So, even on "dry" days, I press into God in obedience to His spiritual principles and know that He is God.

PSALM 30:11–12: "Thou hast turned for me my mourning into dancing: thou hast put off my sackcloth, and girded me with gladness; To the end that my glory may sing praise to thee, and not be silent, O Lord my God, I will give thanks unto thee for ever."

I Am My Beloved's

SONG OF SOLOMON 7:10: "I am my beloved's, and his desire is toward me."

How often in Scripture the Lord speaks of His relationship with the believer in terms of the marriage relationship. In The Revelation, Jesus refers to Himself as the bridegroom and to the church as His bride. And so many of the Hebrew words I have searched out have as part of their definition the word *marry*. For instance, the word *inhabits*, used in Psalm 22:3 ("But thou art holy, O thou who **inhabitest** the praises of Israel") has as one of its definitions the word *marry*. In a lovely spiritual analogy of this marriage relationship, the prayers, praise, and worship of the believer are described in Scripture as incense and smoke, and the manifested Presence of the Lord as a cloud of smoke. As the smoky incense of praise and worship ascends to the Lord, the cloud of smoke of the Presence of the Lord descends and the two become one. To me this is a beautiful vision that vividly describes the union He so desires with all of us!

And just as tension develops when something is not quite right in the marriage relationship, the same is true in the communion and union with the Father. Yesterday, as I came to the Lord in my prayer time and began to praise and worship Him, I became acutely uncomfortable about something I had been vaguely sensing all week in my devotional time. I

determined this morning not to let go of the Lord until He
revealed to me what the problem was between us. As I bowed
before Him and told Him that I could not bear anything
between us, not even the subtlest tension, I heard Him say in
that still, small voice within me, "Open your Bible and read
your normal daily reading pattern. I will tell you there what is
wrong between us." Well, I am presently reading in Jeremiah,
so I opened to the place at which I had stopped the previous
day and began to read. When I came to the 23rd and 24th
verses of the ninth chapter of Jeremiah, the Lord said to me,
"This is what is wrong between you and me. Read it slowly." I
began to read, ". . . Let not the wise man glory in his wisdom,
neither let the mighty man glory in his might, let not the rich
man glory in his riches: But let him that glorieth glory in this,
that he understandeth and knoweth me, that I am the Lord
which exercise lovingkindness, judgment, and righteousness,
in the earth: for in these things I delight, saith the Lord." As I
read, I was pricked in my heart. For the past few weeks I have
been diligently working to complete this book on praise and
worship, a very important subject and ministry to God for me.
And yet the Lord revealed to me that I had allowed the **subject**
and the **activity** of Davidic praise and worship to become more
important than the Object of it all. I had allowed it to crowd
Him out! I realized that I had gotten so "busy" with Davidic
praise and worship that it, rather than the Lord, had become
my focal point! You can well imagine the sense of grief and
shame as the Lord revealed this to me.

Again I am reminded of the marital relationship. The essence
of marriage, to me, is how my husband and I relate to one
another in every area of our lives. Sometimes I get so involved
"doing" for my husband and home and all of my other
activities that I take him for granted and forget **him.** (This, of
course, can go both ways.)

Every morning I kiss my husband good-by when he leaves
for the office, or when I leave for an appointment or trip.
Sometimes I am so busy thinking about all the details of my day
that I kiss him without thinking about it. I try to catch myself
when that happens, and I try to catch my husband when it
happens from his side, because we both deserve more from

each other than that. The same thing can happen in our devotional lives. The expression of love can become perfunctory as opposed to the passionate, unquenchable outpouring that comes from our hearts in the Spirit. The Lord certainly communicated that to me yesterday! I had focused so intensely these last few weeks on Davidic praise and worship that I had forgotten, subtly, the Alpha and the Omega. (But even subtly is too much!) He is the beginning of praise. He is the object of praise. And He is the end of praise. I had become so driven to finish this book, that I had not been diligent in tending to my Lord and had begun to take Him for granted. In my eagerness each morning to get started writing, I had been careless with Him.

After He spoke those words to me in my devotional time yesterday, I went to church. It was incredible! The pastor brought forth the same message for the church that the Lord had given me. He warned us about how subtly tradition and self-satisfaction can creep into our lives, no matter how "alive" our relationship with the Lord is. So the Lord confirmed what I had heard in my prayer time earlier. Of course, this called for deep repentance, and as God began to cleanse me, those "walls" came tumbling down! What a joyful time of praise, worship, and communion with God that was! And what a wonderful morning it was for the entire church.

And what a marvelous work God has done in my life! To have come, by His grace, from a nervous, depressed, fearful, insecure, neurotic, hopeless human being to a person born of God, filled with His Spirit, overflowing with the rivers of living waters, full of joy, peace, hope, patience, love, gentleness, faith, temperance, and great concern for others, is an absolute miracle of God. He very sovereignly brought me into Davidic praise and worship, which has brought me into His Presence. There the shackles and bonds that had been loosed but were still a shadow in my life are being taken away. There I am finding greater and greater liberty of faith. There I am finding my desires being conformed to His. There I am finding more and more fulfillment for all those desires, hopes and dreams each day. There I am learning to hope His hopes and dream His dreams bigger and bigger. There I have found my true love in all His splendor and grandeur, and there I shall continue to grow in all of this by His grace. Wow!

It is the desire of the Lord to do this for each of His children. He is looking for willing hearts. He is looking for the heart of David in us. How quickly He responds to a heart like that. If you are not yet a worshiper in spirit and in truth, join me. God will meet you, just as He met me. He is calling to us, "Come with me . . . my bride" (Song of Sol. 4:8 RSV.) And He is waiting to hear us respond, "Come, my beloved, let us go . . ." (Song of Sol. 7:11).

Since there has been such a strong focus on Davidic praise and worship for much of this book, it seems a strong emphasis on Him, the Alpha and the Omega, is what my heart is yearning for as I close. He is our Lord. Without Him there would be no praise. He is Yahweh, the great I Am That I Am. He is eternal. He has always been and will always be. He is omniscient. He knows every sparrow that falls and every hair on my head. He knows all things in my life and yours. No thought or deed is hidden from Him. He is omnipotent. His power is limitless. Nothing is impossible with Him. No request is too large or too small. He is omnipresent. He is working in every life, wooing us and drawing us to Himself. He is performing wonders too mighty for words in the lives of His children all over the world, and all at the same time. He is not limited in any way—not in time, nor space, nor power, nor wisdom, nor knowledge.

He is merciful. There is no sinner too lost, no sin too dark to be forgiven (except blaspheming the Holy Spirit). He is faithful. What He says, He does. What He has promised, He will perform. He does not lie. He runs us down, even when we are running away from Him. He is just. He never makes a mistake. He is never unfair. He is love. Nothing can win His love and nothing can prevent it. It is unconditional to the believer, but it is conditioned upon faith in Jesus Christ. However, in His love for His creation, He lovingly works in the life of the unbeliever as well to draw him/her to Himself. And His love is tough love. He reproves and chastens us for righteousness and holiness. He is holy. There is no sin in Him, and He cannot look upon sin. He is "high and lifted up." He is exalted above measure.

His arm is strong. His hand is mighty. He scatters His enemies with His mighty arm. Righteousness and justice are the foundation of His throne. Lovingkindness and truth go before Him. Faithfulness surrounds Him. The heavens praise His wonders. All of creation praises Him.

Beloved friend, love the Lord, your God, with all your heart, and with all your soul, and with all your mind, and with all your strength. Love Him with an intense, passionate, burning, heart-throbbing love, the flames of which burn hotter, higher, and brighter with each passing day. Let us surrender our hearts to the one purpose of the constant pursuit of God. With singleness of eye, let us stir ourselves up to take hold of Him. The bridegroom waits for His spotless bride. Let us "press toward the mark for the prize of the high calling of God in Christ Jesus."

Father, we cast ourselves at your feet. You are the Lord God Almighty, Who keeps covenant from everlasting to everlasting. We acknowledge You as the God above all gods. You are exalted above all the heavens and the earth. There is no one like You, Lord. You are King, God!!! Supreme in your authority. Unquestionable in your sovereignty. Majestic in your splendor. Unparalleled in your greatness. Limitless in your power. Infinite in your wisdom and your knowledge. Absolute in your justice. Magnificent in your splendor. Dazzling in your beauty. Ingenious in your creativity. Timeless in your existence. Terrible in your wrath. Unsearchable in your understanding. Indescribable in your tenderness. Unfathomable in your love. Matchless in your grace. Unswerving in your faithfulness. Unending in your mercy. Blazing in your glory. Awesome in your holiness. Pristine in your purity. Fascinating in your personality. God!!! God!!! God!!! O, how our hearts leap within us as we look at You and say, "O for grace to love You more, coming from the knowledge of Who You are." God!!! We declare how little we know of what You are really like. To know You is to love You! To know You is to run to obey You! To know You is to understand You. To know You is to pant and thirst and hunger to know You more, that we may more effectively make You known. Meet our deepest needs by giving us a far greater revelation of Who You are. Thank You that You will. In Jesus' name and by the power and through the person of the Holy Spirit to

Whom we honor and submit, Who alone can bring light, and life and truth from the Father's heart to ours. Amen. *

If we do not meet in this life, I look forward to standing with you, my brother or sister, before the throne of God, worshiping our Lord in spirit and in truth for eternity. Until then, may His kingdom come within you, may His will be done within you, may you praise and worship **in earth as it is in heaven** both now and forevermore. I love you.

HABAKKUK 3:17–19: "Although the fig tree shall not blossom, neither shall fruit be in the vines; the labour of the olive shall fail, and the fields shall yield no meat; the flock shall be cut off from the fold, and there shall be no herd in the stalls; **yet I will rejoice in the Lord, I will joy in the God of my salvation.** The Lord God is my strength, and he will make my feet like hinds' feet, and he will make me walk upon mine high places. . . ."

---

*I thank my sister and most beloved teacher, Joy Dawson, for all of the superlatives in praise of God.

Appendix

Earlier I mentioned two men of God whose writings have greatly influenced my life. They are A. W. Tozer and Andrew Murray. Both of these men's books have been very important to me; they have made me hungry and thirsty to know God. I recommend them highly, particularly Tozer's *The Knowledge of the Holy* (Harper & Row), *The Pursuit of God* (Tyndale), *I Talk Back to the Devil* (Cornerstone Paperbacks), and *Worship—The Missing Jewel of the Evangelical Church* (Christian Publications). I am sure all of Tozer's books are excellent, but those are the ones I have read. I hope to read them all. Andrew Murray's devotional book *God's Best Secrets* (Zondervan) is marvelous and his *Abide in Christ* (Fleming H. Revell) is incredibly inspirational. Graham Truscott has ministered to me on Davidic praise and worship through his books *The Power of His Presence* and *Every Christian's Ministry*. His books can be purchased by writing World Map, 900 N. Glenoaks, Burbank, California 91502. *The Tabernacle of David* by Kevin J. Conner is another fine and helpful book on the subject of praise and worship. It can be purchased by writing Bible Temple–Conner Publications, 7626 N.E. Glisan Street, Portland, Oregon 97214. Also, Judson Cornwall's book *Let Us Praise*, published by Logos, gives many additional insights into the subject of praise and worship in the Word of God. And, of course, **read your Bible.** It is the book I recommend the most!